THE ANCIENT HISTORY OF THE NEWBOLD REVEL VILLAGES IN WARWICKSHIRE FROM 1066 TO 1750

To Delia & Jeffery.

Kind Thoughts & Best Wishes

Colin & Jennifer

RESEARCHED AND COMPILED
BY

COLIN COOK

Published by Colin Cook

Publishing partner: Paragon Publishing, Rothersthorpe

ISBN 978-1-78222-027-5

Book design, layout and production management by Into Print

www.intoprint.net

Printed and bound in UK and USA by Lightning Source

THE REVEL STORY

THE FRONTISPIECE AND QUEEN PICTURE 4
INTRODUCTION 5
BRINKLOW 7
CHURCHOVER 19
CESTERSOVER 27
EASENHALL........................31
FENNY NEWBOLD 33
HARBOROUGH MAGNA 35
MONKS KIRBY 43
PAILTON 55
STREET ASHTON 61
STRETTON UNDER FOSSE........................63
WALTON 65
BROCKHURST 67
WILLEY 69
NEWNHAM PADDOX........................77
POVERTY IN MEDIEVAL TIMES 79
17C. MAP 80
ANCIENT TERMS EXPLAINED........................83
PRINCESS ELIZABETH AT COOMBE THE BLOODLINE ..85
THE MONARCHS FROM 1066 TO 1700........................86
SIR THOMAS MALORY........................87
LORD OF THE MANOR........................89

THE ANCIENT HISTORIES OF THE REVEL VILLAGES IN WARWICKSHIRE.

TO COMMEMORATE THE DIAMOND JUBILEE OF
HER MAJESTY QUEEN ELIZABETH SECOND
2012

`BRINKLOW

MONKS KIRBY

CHURCHOVER

WILLEY

HARBOROUGH
MAGNA

PAILTON

EASENHALL

STRETTON

Researched and
Compiled
By
Colin Cook

The Newbold Revel
(The Revel)

This Booklet commemorates the Diamond Jubilee on 4th, June 2012 of Her Majesty Queen Elizabeth 11, with a collection of the Ancient histories of those villages within the area known as THE REVEL. Bringing the knowledge of the Heritage of these places to all, in one document, that it is hoped, will make interesting reading.

This is a non-profit making collection of researched history from the coming of the Normans up to the Hanoverians. This information has been collected from all the official resources listed below.

A glance at the map shows the triangulation of the two Roman Roads and the profitable topography being the ideal area for settlement (the Anglo Saxons had done for generations).

How the places were distributed for ownership in the Norman military manner of liability is a trifle confusing at times, with the terms of reference hard to understand.

It does reveal the way that land today is built on the basic system of those bygone days. The Earl of Denbigh is still the Lord of the Manor today.

It also allows the reader to become aware of the hard and difficult way that life and the ways of making a living, hung on the structure and definition of ownership.

This your HERITAGE and this is the story of how those places have been developed over the centuries in the places you know today, there have been many interested enquiries of how the place names came about, and this is an attempt to collate these in a way that will make it easy to understand.

The commemoration also has a strong significance for Her Majesty Queen Elizabeth 11, when you become aware that there was another Princess Elizabeth, daughter of King James the First who lived for five years at Coombe Abbey, who later became the Queen of Bohemia; known as The Winter Queen, it was her last daughter Sophie, who married George The Duke of Hanover, her first son came to England in 1714 as our King George the first and brought the Hanoverian line to the English throne. Her Genes are deeply within the Queens today. (See line of Succession)

With acknowledgements to;

Jack Tipper who designed the Celtic borders and took the photographs

David Williams - Kings and Queens of England

A.C. Fox Davies - Art of Heraldry

Tim Graham - Jubilee

John Morris - The Domesday Book

L. F. Salzman - Victorian History of Warwick

Marie Louise Bruce - Usurper King

Tilley & Warwick - Church Bells of Warwick

Arthur Mee - Warwickshire

British online history - Warwickshire

Roy Bourne - History of Pailton

Lastly with thanks to my Wife Jenny who proof read this.

Brinklow

(Bryncaslow)

The name Brinklow appears in the Domesday Book, but only as a Hundred and then called BOMELAW, interpreted as Brinklow.

That the dwellings hereabouts were within the place called **Smite**, (now a depopulated place) from the stream close called Smite.

This place has many explanations as to the derivation of the name.

Quote; from the Anglo Saxon and Victorian History as,

This place hath its name doubtless from that eminent Tumuli whereon the Keep or Watch Tower of the Castle, which long ago was there, did stand, but whether it was because this little hill, by us was termed a Low or Law, on the edge of a Brink of a natural ascent of the country hereabouts. From the British word would appear as Brink which is the same with Colis in latin, 'tis hard to say, leave it best for the reader to say the name. Unquote.

The Anglo Saxon Chronicles, Quote, In the year 890, K. Arthur fortified the Low here to protect locals, using it as a Touters signal tower, to warn of enemies to use smoke by day and fire by night. Also in 1050 K. Edward the Confessor, is said to have raised the earthworks and fortified it further for villagers to withdraw to as will be needed. Wherein a chieftain named Brynca was in hold for him, (a hill in their language was a low or law). So for some time now it been accepted as Bryncas low or Brinklow.

OVERLORDSHIP HISTORY reads; in 1086, it was in E. Alberics hands and held it for the King, thence to Earl of Leicester, and by him to Nigel de Albany. Father of Roger de Mowbray, who held it for the Earl for one Knights fee. Who raised the first parish chapel in 1101. The incumbent was known as Samson de Albanie. Who with the church at Smite and the chapel at Brinklow was placed in the hands of Kenilworth Priory.

After a short period in the hands of Earl Aubrey, it passed to Robert, Count of Meulan, and so to the Earldom of Leicester, and afterwards to Earl of Lancaster. In 1275 the Earl of Leicester had the right to hold a Court in Brinklow twice a year and had an assize of bread and ale in 1275 the Earl of Leicester, also had a twice yearly view of a Frankpledge. The subsequent tenancy of this very lucrative holding, i.e. Covered 50 acres and meadowland, also 4 acres, and a mill, with 12 villiens, (free men) 6 villagers, 2 slaves, and 37 ploughs, and all their property.

It is important to note that when the land holdings changed hands so did all the people therein, they were sold with every thing else that they had as though they were the goods and chattels that went with the sale.

Sometimes this could turn out to be a disaster, should the new tenant be a cruel demanding one, and often would only increase the hardship and poverty already there. The villiens were allowed a small patch of land to breed their small animals and grow vegetables and to provide for the harsh winter that would always follow. This could be made worse if the tenant was due to entertain on a big scale and with insufficient food to go on their table to impress and allow them to gorge, they would instruct the Verderer to collect from the poor villagers all that was needed for the table, in many cases leaving the

St John's at night.

populace destitute with nothing for the winter. All that the Lord allowed was for them to go out and get what little they could find with their shepherds crook, and billhook and gather all that was within arms reach. (Hence the expression by bill and crook!.)

The Manors

From the 12th century the principal tenancy, was in the hands of the Mowbrays, (it was the grandfather who went to do battle with Henry Lancaster, he was exiled). His relative Roger de Mowbray was holding Brinklow for the Earl of Leicester by the service of one knight's fee. (read Harbrough Magna story)

When in 1201 a lawsuit involving the values of Brinklow was brought by William de Stuteville against William de Mowbray, the matter dated back to 1106, when after the battle of Tinchebrai Robert Grondebeouf, William De Stutevilles great grandfather, a partisan of Robert of Normandy, lost his Barony to Neil de Aubigny, great grandfather of William de Mowbray. Roger de Mowbray had compensated Robert de Stuteville with Kirby Moorside (Yorks) for 10 knights fees, during the reign of K. Henry 11, but William de Stuteville did not recognise this as it was not confirmed in the Kings court. As a result of his suit he was granted, in return for relinquishing his claim to his great grandfathers Barony. The decision was £12 rent and an additional 9 knights fees. A large part of this extra compensation would have come from Brinklow, and was considered as worth £12 yearly a tidy sum in those days. In 1218 William de Stuteville. Williams Nephew was confirmed in possession of the Manor and had the right to hold a weekly market in Brinklow on Mondays and an annual fair on St. Margarets day. Granted to his Father Nicholas, by King John. Fairs provided a good source of income from produce and stallholders. By 1240 another grant of a weekly market in Brinklow on Tuesdays, was made to Stephen de Segrave. This however was in error, as no Segrave connexion can be traced.

By this time the Brinklow 'housed' population was considered as high as Barnacle this was held in very high esteem both in value and lifestyle for that time.

Joan de Stuteville married with Hugh Wake of Liddell the manor came to her son Baldwin in 1276. Then in 1298 John Wake held one knights fee in Brinklow from the Earl of Lancaster by homage and scutage, his tenants coming to view the frankpledge.

In the late 13th and early 14th centuries the principal of these tenants was the Whittlebury family. Aubrey de Wytleburi was enfeoffed by Joan de Stuteville in an estate in Brinklow to hold yearly by rendering one Sore Sparrow Hawk. Gilbert de Wittleburi in 1282 was continuing to hold same rendering yearly for yet another sore sparrow hawk! Or 2s yearly as a knights fee pertaining to the manor of Kirby Moorside. In 1316 John de Wittlebury was in possession, he gave it to his son Aubrey and his first wife Alice intail; later John made a fresh grant of Brinklow to Aubrey and his second wife Joan. In 1341 Aubrey held the manor. Note; the name Whittlebury seems to have several forms of spelling in the settlements.

Benefactors to Brinklow

Three years later William de Thorp, probably a kinsman received a license to alienate the manor of Brinklow in mortain to the abbot and convent of Combe, the yearly value being stated as 66s 8d without a watermill and pond in the tenancy of Sir John Ryvel, later his wife and son John agreed to give the mill and pond on Sir John's death to Combe. At the inquisition preceding this grant, William de Thorp was stated to hold the manor belonging to Thomas Wake of Liddell, who held it of John de Mowbray, who held it of Earl of Lancaster.

Still further alienations of land in Brinklow to the Abbot of Combe in 1347 and 1350. In the latter year the Abbots was holding one knights fee of Thomas Wake of Liddell. As late as 1495 Robert Wittlebury a descendant of Aubrey, made a quitclaim of the manor to Combe Abbey. It is recorded that the monastery of Combe abbey was the richest in Warwickshire at this time.

The changes of ownership of all the Combe holdings were changed by marriages in the 14th century. In 1325 the marriage of Margaret, the daughter, and heiress of Thomas Wake to Edmund Earl of Kent. The overlord ship then came to his earldom.

Brinklow was one of the manors in dower to Elizabeth, widow of John, 3rd Earl of Kent, it was still in her possession when she died in 1411. It was then stated to have been granted by K. Edward 3rd to Edmund Earl of Kent's father in law. The marriage of John the 5th Lord Mowbray in 1349 with Elizabeth Segrave, the daughter and heiress of the Duchess of Norfolk, brought a similar change in the next higher tenancy. (Note all this was still in the overlord ship of the Earl Mowbray.)

In 1399 Thomas first Duke of Norfolk held two and a quarter knight's fee in Warwickshire, so that in 1462 the third Duke of Norfolk, held one and one tenth fees in Brinklow. In 1539 the Duchess of Richmond was granted the tenancy for life, she died in 1557. It was then granted to Robert Lee of Horton, and also to Anthony Throckmorton of Chastleton, combined with Great Addington Northants, was said to be one knight's fee in value. They both obtained a license to grant the manor of Brinklow to William Dawes, his heirs and assigns, to be held in chief.

Part of the parish and including the site of the Castle was in the hands of Sir Arthur Gregory of Stivichall in 1626. However in 1654 what became known as the manor was in the hands of John Gregory. This had been a frankpledge in 1636 to John Williams the younger and Simon Edolhpe that another manor in Brinklow came to Sir Fulwar Skipwith family in 1628, confirmed in 1707, and again in 1731. The Skipwith Baronetcy became extinct in 1790. Thomas Skipwith, a distant cousin, was a vouchee in recovering the manor in 1850, and Brinklow manor was in the joint hands of Sir Grey Skipwith and A.F. Gregory of Stivichall.

An interesting aside; With the railway coming to Coventry it had to cross the lands of Gregory ,Hood by a building a bridge, the families agreed provided the coats of arms of family should be shown on each side of the bridge. The road became known as the Coat of Arms Bridge Road, it still has the arms on the bridge today!

Brinklow which gave its name to the Hundred latterly became known as Knightlow was a large village, by 1730 there were 300 dwellings there this density was high for a rural place. Containing a large amount of alehouses to oblige the thirsts, and had to be reduced since it caused disruption in the working persons in the village.

There was another manor in Brinklow that had a different story of belonging to Mowbray in 1201, he passed it to William Stuteville who retained a Simon de Cornuba to hold it as one knights fee. Which went to Monks Kirby and given to John Mowbray of Axholme priory in 1361, which was absorbed by the Carthusians in 1415. At the dissolution those lands in Brinklow were assigned in life to Thomas Mannyng Bishop of Ipswich, with the remainder to Charles Brandon, Duke of Suffolk.

One tenth of a knight's fee was held of Thomas de Bray in 1298. Another fraction was in the hands of Thomas de Grey. In both cases the Mowbrays were the Overlords.

This was identical with the tenth fee held by John the Duke of Norfolk in 1461.

So that a messuage of land in Brinklow was devised by will in 1625 by Thomas Wale citizen of London, to provide a school master and usher in the school at Monks Kirby, and the school to be free to the children of Brinklow!

The extent of acreage appertaining to Brinklow is not clear, but viewing the above, knights fees, and several manors and parts of manors, and the usage in value they must have been quite extensive, not shown on those early maps.

Plan of St. John's

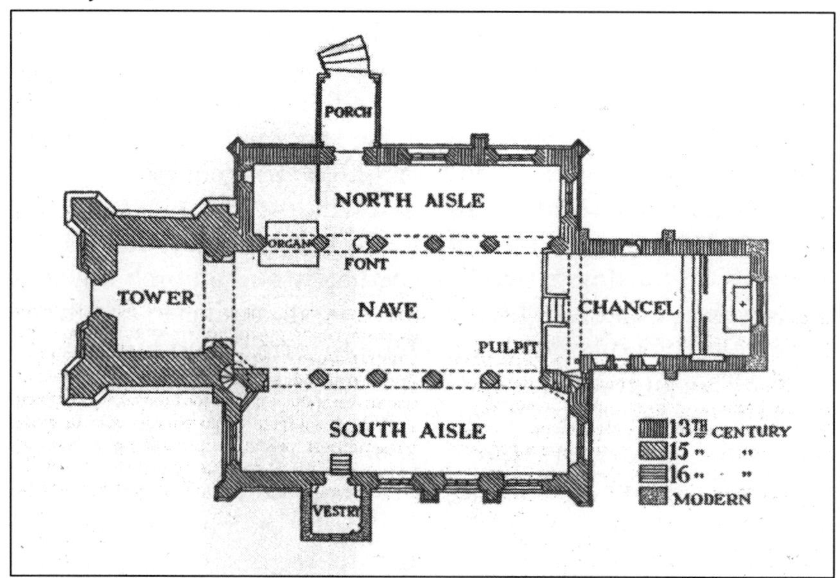

The Church
Saint John the Baptist

Previously stated there was a chapel here in 1101 with an incumbent Simon de Albanie

Who also held a church at Smite, supposedly there are only the masonry remains of the chapel within the church today. These records indicate that there was a chapel here at that time. The Tower and South aisle are 15th, the rest is 16th to modern. The Chancel and North aisle and staircase to the rood loft are 13th century.

The Tower and South aisle are 15th the rest is 16th to modern.

Great care and devotion has been taken on modernisation and the amazing unusual feature of the rise from the nave to the chancel of 12 feet, makes this church unique, and tells the story of the additions by the end of the 15/16th centuries, the south porch has been converted into a vestry. The north side still has a door and made into the Porch.

The CHANCEL is built of a mixture of limestone, sandstone bricks and rubble. A steep pitched roof with a finial and rebuilt buttresses. The east window is modern with three lights, with a hood- mould and head-stops. The south side has a central buttress, and two restored lancet windows, with a narrow doorway between them. The lancet window divided to form a low side window. The south aisle is built of red sandstone ashlar, with a plinth of one splay, stepped down to conform to the slope. The wall here is diminished in thickness by a weathered off set at sill level. It has a low pitched roof with a low parapet, has a moulded projection on a moulded stringcourse. The east gable is light by a restored traceried window of three cinquefoil lights under a moulded four centered head. The south wall has a buttress at the angle, two intermediately and a porch towards the western end, it is lighted by three lights similar to one in the west wall. The porch has been rebuilt to form the entrance to the vestry. The south door has a four centred head under a square head, it is mutilated. The west end is similar to the east, but the coping is carried up to a lean-to instead of a gable. The buttress is splayed at the angle is diagonal and pointed. The north side is made of rubble similar to the chancel and has a lean to roof, a battlemented parapet with trefoil panelled pinnacles with crocketed finials. Originally there were two pinnacles of which only the bosses remain. The north side has diagonal buttresses on the angle. One intermediate, and to the west is a porch. The porch is timber framed with a tiled roof, with a pair of modern doors, the front retains its timbering, the front having a heavy moulded frame and a four-centred head, carved spandrels and lintel, and a timber framed gable. In the centre is a hood mould with shield and three crossed swords (said to be of Clarke 17th cent)

THE TOWER. Built of light coloured sandstone ashlar with a moulded plinth and battlemented parapet on a coved string- course. It rises in four stages, diminished at each stage by weathered offsets on the north and south. At the angles there are diagonal buttresses rising in five stages, splayed off. One has gabled trefoiled niches. The west doorway, in a deep moulded splay, is of red sandstone under a square head, flanked by two tiers roll moulded panels. Above the doorway is a tall pointed traceried window of three lights and a hood mould, in the second stage is a clock dial, recently gilded. The tower staircase is in the south west angle, with a loop light to each stage and a square- headed doorway opening on to the aisled roof. The belfry is lighted on each face by a traceried window of two lights, and the ringing chamber by similar windows on the north and south.

Internally the floor is of modern tiles, laid to a continuous fall from east to west, replacing the steps shown by the stepping down of arcades and windows. Walls are plastered.

THE CHANCEL has four steps from the nave, and three to the altar in addition to the slope of the floor. The east wall has a modern dado of embossed tiles, and the window a segmental rear pointed arch. East end of the south wall is a shallow recess with square heads, and the doorway a segmental pointed rear arch. The roof has hammer beams, and carved stone Gorbels, under the chancel arch has twin trusses with pierced panels on slender stone shafts with carved capitals.

THE NAVE has a roof of 18th/19th century with curved trusses resting on moulded timbered corbels, displaying the delightful coloured shields of benefactors of the church over the ages. Both arcades have five bays of pointed arches, of two splayed orders, supported on lozenge shaped roll moulded pillars, thinning out on the mouldings. At the junction of the south arcade with the chancel there is a circular stair up to a square headed doorway, which gave access to a rood, half way up there is a pointed opening to the aisle. It is lighted from the side with two windows squared.

The Chancel arch is a modern pointed one with an inscription in latin to Christmas, resting on a floriated corbel. The tower has a pointed arch of two splays to the tower and three to the nave, the inner order supported on three quarter responds with moulded capitals and bases. The arch is of red sandstone with capitals of a lighter stone, and on the tower side in the apex is a carving of an angel. The south west angle is corbelled out in three steps for the tower staircase, the upper step being trefoiled, and below is a square headed door way. The pulpit and reading desk are of modern stone.

The South aisle has a low pitched open roof of five bays with moulded members with carved bosses in the centre of tie beams. Possibly dating from the 15/16th century; forming a Ladies Chapel dating from the 15th century the boarding and some rafters are modern. The trusses resting on stone corbels on the south wall, and the north wall arcade pillars are on the carried up with pillars. It carries a memorial tablet to a past incumbent dating 1680-1734. At the east end, the north east angle is splayed to accommodate the rood. The windows have hollowed mounted reveals with centred rear arches, the window to the east having the arch extended eastwards and carried down to form a recess. The east wall has an offset at sill level with a chamfered stone capping, and the window reveals are carried down as a recess. In the east window are some fragments of very early coloured glass Possibly Norman and depicting two chalices and part of a canopy. What was the south porch has been converted to a Vestry, the glass depicts Our Lord carrying the cross, and the good Samaritans.

The North aisle has a lean to roof of five bays, of which two retain the original their original moulded members, dating from the 15th century. The trusses are supported on stone corbels on the north wall and on square blocks of stone as capitals to the outer roll moulding of the arcade pillars. Over the door is a painted coat of arms of George IV. The Font lead lined is built in with the west side of the north arcade pillar opposite the door.

It is of stone is of 15th century, with octagonal stem and base paterae of roses. There is a 17th century oak chest with three hasps of the time when all three designees had to be present. In the centre and east windows are more fragments of early coloured glass, depicting a peacock, a castle and two small birds. These specimens of glass are rare dating before stained glass, and long before English glass was made. The two manual organ, is dated 1873. It forms a chapel of remembrance to all Souls.

The Tower has a window with splayed reveals, and a rear arch of two splayed orders; the recess is carried down to include the doorway. In the chancel are a number of 18th,19th century memorials. Displayed is a frame showing the names of those shields displaying the families.

There are six bells. Five dated 1705 by Joseph Smith of Edgbaston. The Six is recent.

ADVOWSON. Brinklow was originally a Chapelry of Smite. This was granted with the parent church, in the reign of Henry 1ST, by Samson de Albenei with the consent of Roger de Mowbray to the Priory of Kenilworth. The patronage continued with that house just before the dissolution (see Previous manors) The value of the rectory was £4 in 1291 and £17 10s in 1535.

CHARITIES; William Edwards by will dated 9 June 1789, gave to the minister, churchwardens, and overseers of Brinklow £500, the yearly interest to be distributed in bread to the amount of 5s. 6d. Every Sunday at church to the most deserving and necessitous poor of the parish. Any remaining sum is given in bread on Christmas day. Mary Baker by will dated December 1721 gave £20 to the minister and churchwardens of Brinklow, to be laid out in bread on the Sunday after Christmas day and on Whitsunday given to poor persons regularly attending church: £10 of which was lost by the insolvency commission. The amount of these charities still stands today and varies with the sterling valuation. Ann Brierly by will of the 16th July 1863 gave £25 to the rector the income of which to provide coal and to be distributed on December 21 to the necessitous widows residing in the parish. The income of which amounts to 12s, 4d. Mary Ferguson who died in 1862 she bequeathed to the rector and church wardens £100, interest amounting then to £2 12s, to be given at Christmas amoung the deserving widows. Elizabeth

Frances Lyne Hill by will dated 29 July 1925 gave to the rector and church wardens £500, income to be distributed to the deserving poor of the parish. The annual income was £14 6s 4d. The Rev. Thomas Muston (a tablet to him is on the south wall of the south aisle) dated 30 September 1729, certain property in Foleshill with the annual payment of 20s, to the minister of Brinklow for the use of the poor of the parish, special regard to those who frequent the church. Rent charge was redeemed in 1926 valued at £40, 3s, producing annual income of 20s. James Hancox by will dated 1752 devised land called Potters close to trustees to dispose of the rents and profits among the poor of the parish. This land was sold in 1947 and the proceeds of sale were invested. Alice Ansley indenture on 11 January 1635, charged certain property in Brinklow the payments yearly of 10s be paid for the repair of the church on Good Friday. Thomas Wale by codicil dated 19 April 1625 ordained that the Mayor and Aldermen of Coventry yearly bestow from the rents of certain property devised to them the sum of 40s. to the church wardens and overseers of the church of Brinklow to be distributed to the poor of the parish.

Churchover

(Churchwaure)

It is thought that the name in Saxon times was 'Waga'. He was the chieftain that owned the land; Waga also gave his name to Wootton Wawen. In 1086 the lands were in the hands of Robert de Stafford, continued in the hands of Stafford. Two thirds of a knight's fee being held by Robert de Wavra. In 1166 as part of four knights fees which Robert Fitz Otes held of the Staffords. Roger in this time was apparently Roger de Waver, who in the time of K. Henry II 1154 confirmed the gift to Combe Abbey a gift of 96 acres and a Grangia this was made by his father son of Seward de Waver, who in this time named the Village Church Waver.

The name waure is another name for others or overs, and a church was founded here by Rogerus de Waure, and to distinguish him from other Waure's they named him as Rogerus de Church-Waure and passed the gift fees of 96 acres to Combe,the village became known as Church Waure, and later known as ChurchOver.

The other overs (Waures) locally were, CestersOver, BrownsOver.

The Manors

In 1223, a problem arose over a mill worth 2s in the Domesday book.

Cecily former wife of William de Shirewode, who husband gave up married life to become a monk at Combe Abbey. She wanted to claim one third of the mill in a dower to her, in this time it was worth £1, a

third only was granted. The mill was handed to Churchover in 1600, and was not heard of after this.

The manor seems to have come into the hands of two co-heiresses before 1280, when Elizabeth, wife of John Beneyt, and Joan wife of Thomas Dadelinton, shared the advowson of the church. Elizabeth conveyed her share to John, son of Simon de Shirford. In 1292 Richard de Stapleford and Joan his wife held a moiety of the manor in her own right. John de Shirford and Ralph de Morton held the manor they were Lords in 1316.

The Advowson and presumably the manor in 1323; were held by Thomas Ireys and Alice Stafford. In 1330 the John de Hampton granted a revision to Thomas, son of Geoffery Ireye of Ansty. In 1332 the Ireys conveyed their moeiity of the manor to Master Robert de Stratford (later Bishop of Chichester and Chancellor) In 1337 John de Shirford conveyed one moiety to Simon, Vicar of Nuneaton, and then jointly assigned in 1343 to Phillip Purefoy he died in 1468 and it was seized of the moiety of the manor which he left to his wife Isabel for life, and to his son John aged 10 in tail. The Purefoys held land here since 1227, and was the biggest taxpayer here in 1332, and they continued to hold the manor until 1566, when it was sold to Sir Thomas Leigh. In 1602 it was sold by William Leigh to William Bond, who in turn sold it to William Dixwell, after which it descended in to the manor of Coton.

It seems quite probable that in the de Stratford's time it was intended to convey the moiety of the Ireys to Kenilworth Priory, as in 1333 license was granted for the aleiniation of it in mortain to the priory. So from this time and until the dissolution the living was given alternatively by the Purefoys and to Kenilworth Priory.

There were many tenants at this time since the living yielded £4 12s 8d in rents, these dwellings consisted of the manor of ChurchOver at this time. Somehow it came into the hands of Humphrey Burnaby and his wife Cecily who sold it to William Dixwell (his mothers nephew) in 1669

The 96 acres of land given to Combe Abbey were added to by Alice Duas in 1288 and was of 6 messuages and 16 virgates of land, and were very profitable producing

£3 11s and a mill 20s,and 6s for court pleas, (note. manorial

Holy Trinity Churchover.

courts active at this time) also a large farm producing £5 from stock! In K. Richard the 11's time the monks were reputed to have increased their income with 6 messuages and 155 acres of land here. All this went to the Duchess of Richmond after the dissolution, and she alieniated the manor to William Dixwell, who already had a part tenancy. He died on 1581 and passed it to his son Humphey on his marriage to Helen Lowe and the manor descended for 200 years with Coton. It was then known as Churchover and Coton.

In 1774 it was passed to Abraham Grimes, who built Coton House, and his son Henry Grimes was lord of the manor in 1850. Somehow the manor came into the hands of Francis Arkwright, he died in 1915, the advowson passed to Mrs. Arthur James, JP. Who was lady of the Manor in 1936.

The Church

The Holy Trinity consists of a Chancel, with vestry and organ chamber on the south side, nave, north and south aisles, south porch, west tower, and spire.

The south arcade, south door, and west tower are the only medieval portions of the present building; the remainder dates from 1896, when the church was rebuilt, and mainly in the 14th century style. The architect was Basset Smith.

Before this there was no chancel arch, the walls of the chancel and nave being continuous; they were probably of 13th century. The Apse and south porch were modern additions.

The south arcade is of three bases. The late 13th centiury octagonal pillars were originally of grey stone with signs of modern repairs as do the moulded capitals and bases, the two centered arches, has two chamfered orders, they do not fit the capitals, the outer order projecting out over the abacus.

The doorway in the south aisle is 13th century. It has a moulded two centered head and in the jambs two narrow shafts with conjoined capitals, there is a defaced hood mould with defaced hood stops. The rear arch is modern.

The 15th century west tower is of small coursed limestone rubble with angled buttress's, both on a firm base of Ashlar. At the angles are narrow buttresses of four offsets, and at the south east angle there is a stair-vice. Both tower and buttresses are built upon a heavy base of ashlar with a moulded plinth. The three segmental tower has chamfered orders. The west window has three pointed lights with mullions and spandrels on a four centred head; the middle light is cinqefoiled those

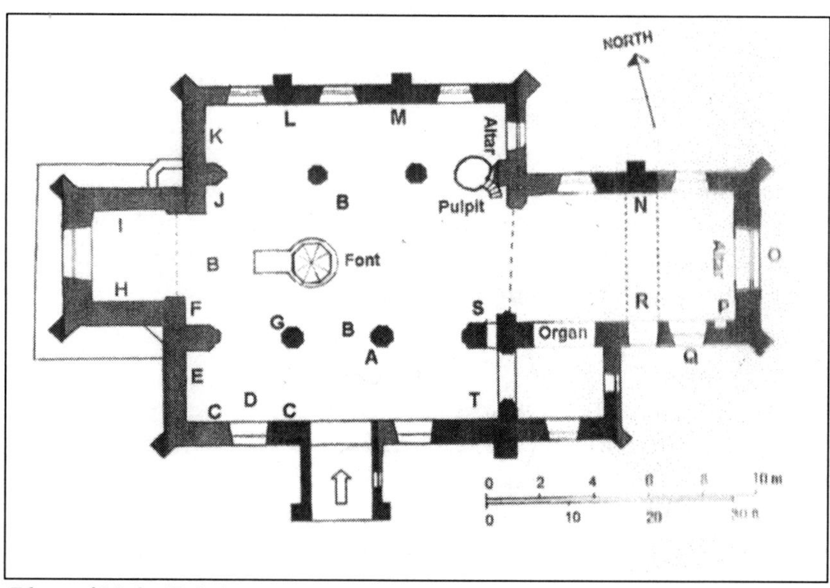

Plan of Holy Trinity.

Memorials to the Dixworth family.

flanking it are trefoiled. The original head and tracery were of red sandstone, now showing signs of cement work. The round headed rear arch has splayed jambs and shows signs of Axe dressing. The second stage north, west and south faces have square windows.

In the third stage, the bell chamber, there are in each of the four faces they have square windows with two pointed trefoiled lights with blind square heads.

The parapet recessed angles being flushed with the sides, indicated by a string-course. The Octagonal spire is devoid of architectural ornament; with two sets of plain lights. Both tower and steeple were restored in 1911.

On the west wall on the north side is a monument erected in 1641 to Charles Dixwell of Coton and his wife Abigail. Two flat marble pilasters with Corinthian capitals support an architrave frieze with strap work and a moulded cornice. Beneath the kneeling figures of Charles and Abigail Dixwell face each other with a pre-dieu between them.

Below them are busts of four sons and one daughter. On the west a wall of the south aisle is a monument to Humphrey and Ann Dixwell, their daughter Mary and husband Robert Price. There is an entablature with architrave, decorated frieze, and cornice carried on three fluted Corinthian columns, linked by two emphasised keystones to two shallow semi circular-headed recesses with two pairs of kneeling figures, each face to face and a pre-dieu between them.

Below monument and near the respond of the arcade is a much worn and mutilated slab of a foliated cross, probably from some ancient cross or corbel.

Note; one tablet bears the name of John Dixwell and was he who was a signatory to the signing of the death warrant of K. Charles 1st it cost him dearly when K. Charles 2nd came to the throne for he had to flee the country and went to the Americas and he became one of the founder members of Conneticut USA. Churchovers Elizabethan Chalice was taken to Conneticut USA, to commemorate the founding.

Not used for sometime is a Bier for a coffin or casket it must be later than the 17th century, because coffins did not come into use by the public until then.

There is a story is of a tablet for Alexander Dixwell, the words and indentations fill with water in certain humid conditions, just this tablet none of the others! There is another wall memorial to William Price but bears no date? The costume is of Tudor design 1660 app.

The 12th century Font is a truncated inverted cone with a roll moulding on the bottom edge, and a cable ornament between roll mouldings on the upper edge. The delightful wooden font cover has a date of 1673, with initials RB and WP.

The pews are Victorian, replacing the old Hanoverian ones, the wood from these was thoughtfully used in the rebuilding.

In the ringing chamber there are some interesting items: a gift for the poor by the Dixwell family, another gave a yard and a half of land, others gave gifts in 1627 £5, 1675 £10, 1690 £5, 1692 £5. Another John Thorp gave £40.0

There are four inscribed bells two 1622 by Watts, another one of 16th century. Also another one of 1803. There is a silver paten dated 1690 and an 18th century chalice with cover. The registers begin in 1658, with a gap until 1721. Miss Mary Benn gave money for a new clock made by Thwaites of London in 1862.

Norman font with cover dated 1673.

King Edward VII, when visiting Coton House whilst on his way north would come into church for services and there were two pews reserved for him. The Chancel screen dated 1951, was presented by her Majesty the Queen Mother in memory of Mrs. Arthur James of Coton House. Who was her God mother.

The Altar and stained glass window, designed by A. Rosenkratz, dedicated to Arthur James and installed by his widow. It shows Christ in Glory, with Angels.

Another window dedicated to the Hon. Lennox Butler and his wife. There is a small communion alcove.

A visit to this church can be very rewarding looking at those fine items and stones on display.

ADVOWSON; The Advowson and rectory remained in the hands of the manor. The church was valued at £5 in 1291 and at £15 in 1535. In 1320 the sheriff seized the chapel into the king's hands because the abbot had for two months failed to perform a service there. This was because his canon Geoffrey Spigneuil had been robbed in here. In 1325 the license was transferred to his conventual church, based on the grounds it was too near Watling Street and a constant haunt of robbers. The endowment of the chantry was two and a half virgates in Holywell, Churchover, and Clifton. But the monks seem to have parted with the land before the dissolution.

CHARITIES; Abigail Harcourt by indenture in 1627 gave certain arable lands, meadows, and arable pasture in the common fields of Churchover on trust that the rents yearly on lady day in the parish church be bestowed on the poor.

The Poor's Estate is an endowment charity source unknown, consists of a piece of a garden in ground known as 'poors yard' in Churchover, together with five cottages built on it. These charities are regulated and the income providing clothing, coals, and necessaries sold at reduced prices, given to those in dire circumstances.

The income came to £59.0 a tidy sum in those days. The Rev. William Benn by will in 1892 bequeathed £500.0 the interest to be for the purchase of flannel blankets, coal, bread to be distributed to the poor of the parish this amounted to £32.10s annually.

CestersOver

Their story begins in the time of Alfred the Great, it is with the Danes on the line of Watling Street. It is suggested this was the place. The Domesday Book quotes this as a place on the river Over (now Swift) crossing at this place was Cester's crossing over. With ten and five hides holding probably covered. Churchover, Brownsover.

The book reads--

Robert holds 5 hides in Cesters Over. Land for 8 ploughs in Lordship 1; 3 slaves 9 villagers and 2 small holders with 5 ploughs, a mill at 2s; meadow,10 and a half acres. The value was and is 40s.

In 1086 Robert held of Geoffrey de Wirce 5 hides in 'Wara'

Later called Waver or CestersOver may have been the place of the family Waver. The history begins with Robert de Waver who held one knights fee here of Neil de Mowbray c1225. and of Richard de Curzun, who held of Roger de Mowbray in 1242. He gave land in Cesters Over to the Abbey of Combe, where he desired to be buried. His son William in 1257 had a grant of a market on Tuesdays in this Manor of Waver, and a yearly fair on the eve, day, and morrow of St James. Cesters Over was big enough to be a Manor at this time.

With the beginning of the Barons war in 1215, Sir William was taken by the Royal forces at Northampton his estates seized and given to Roger de Somery, with whom he compounded for their recovery in 1267 but he died in 1271, and was seized of the manor which was held of Richard de Cursun of Queensborough, his son then 24 in 1307, the order on the manor was reversed and settled on the Waver family.

On his marriage to Alice daughter of Robert Lovett of Newton, subject to the interest of (Williams father) Robert de Waver.

Four members of the Waver family contributed to the subsidy in 1332 at CeastersOver! John and William, each being rated highly at 6s since part at least came back into the hands of the Lovett family at Lipscombe (Bucks). In 1385 granted to William Purefoy the reversion of 12 messuages and 13 virgates of land in CestersOver and Cosford held by John Paraunt and Clemence his wife (who was said to be the mother of William Lovett) for rest of her life. Their grandsons were recorded to have held this in 1432. Again a peculiar twist of property owners, William Broke, son and heir of Ellen Broke of Astwell (Northants) granted his rights in the manor of Henry Waver, citizen of London for life. (this was in unrecorded circumstances), within five years definite releases of moiety of the Manor. William Bate of Melbourn (Derby) made similar releases of his money!

In January 1467 Sir Henry Waver, who was then Sheriff of London, was granted a View of Frankpledge in this Manor with a license to cranellate walls, and Towers there, and to impark 500 acres at either manor of CestersOver or Weavers Marston. However he died two years later, followed by his son in 1478. He left a daughter Christine aged five, this was then seized by the Duchess of Norfolk, who erroneously stated it was of her manor of Melton Mowbray!

Christine married twice first to William Browne secondly to Humphrey Dimmock Christine, never happy in the second marriage turned the tables on the Dimmock family, and on her death in 1545 she passed the estate on her Grandson Edward Browne. Who sold it to Sir Fulke Greville,(in whose family it descended until 1800) George Earl Brooke of Warwick being then Lord. But then it appears to have been in the hands of Robert Arkwright in 1632. After which it was back in the hands of the Greville, then the Brooke family in 1800.

There does not appear to have a record trace after 1800 and what happened to this very prosperous village that was so much sought after and had so many devious dealings with ownership. It had a very historic connection with the Mowbray family who were overlords, and then back to the original Waver family.

The Domesday book reads there is a mention of a Brown at Brownsover, and the extract reads;

Brown holds 2 hides in Brownsover.

Land for 2 ploughs, they are with; 4 villagers, 3 smallholders with 5 ploughs; a mill at 2s; and 2 slaves. A meadow 2 acres. The value was and is 20s.

Note; in the charter of 1077 by Geoffey de Wirce endowing the Abbey of St, Nicholas of Angers the Ville was called Copston and seemed to be the equivalent in size of Monks Kirby which at that time included CestersOver. So that whilst in Monastic hands it was the centre of administration of Copston. But after the dissolution Cestersover became only a member of Monks Kirby!

How it became depopulated and by whom is not clear.

All that can be seen on the map today is the remains of a moat and Cesters Farm.

Easenhall
(Esenhull)

This is another place in the Revel where it can truly be said that there is a record of 'Romano British' dwellings here, found when a Time Team researched and discovered it recorded it all (the layout is now in the British museum,) it was then covered up again. But it is still there!

This site had the ideal situation for early Saxon dwellings, and the pre Saxon 'Coritani' dwelt there, but remains of Saxons have yet to be found. No knight's fees are recorded here. It takes it name as a rise (Hull) of ground and East (esen) from the claim to Monks Kirby, then to Malory then to Cave by heirs general. There were fifty houses there at this time!

The records begin with K.Edward II and wife Isabella.

The lands which William Revel in 1316 settled on his son. Besides Paylington and Feni Newbold, it also included Esenhall and Stretton-sub-Fosse.

Easenhall was partly in the hands of the Beyvilles, a sum of 100s in rents there being held of John, son and heir of Edmund, Earl of Kent, by Lora widow of Richard de Beyville, at her death in 1350, her son Robert being only 5 years old, custody was given to William Peck. No further trace of the Beyvilles has been found. Ownership of the land passes into doubt. It is not known how in 1487 Nicholas Malory was said to have converted 30 acres of arable land in Easenhall to pasture, thus causing six persons and a plough to be unemployed. This is without right of tenancy!

However in 1501 John Smith died holding 3 messuages and 3 virgates of land here worth £6, from Nicholas Malory. When his son died in 1513 the property was large enough to be called a Manor, and was then held by Edward Cave (husband of Nicholas Malory's daughter) and Margery Malory, (Dorothy's sister) The mystery deepens for a Henry Smith son Sir William Smith held the manor and was murdered by his second wife in 1553.

His son Richard who died in 1593, settled the Manor on his daughter Margaret on their marriage to William Littleton, (still the dark deeds continue) by whose father Sir John Littleton 'tricked' him out of the reversion of his estates both here and at Shelford in Burton Hastings. Who then sold Easenhall to Sir John Hale (history records him as infamous of Coventry misdeeds) but on his death in 1609, his son Sir Warwick Hale succeeded him. Easenhall, by then was no longer a Manor, but described as 2 messuages and 440 acres of land became pasture and grazing thus avoiding heavy tax dues.

Of the land that had 50 dwellings at this time, with Villeins, Bordars, and their ploughs and the families that went with them, nothing has been recorded. It is known that this was not a depopulated place.

Fenny Newbold
Later
Newbold Revel

In 1086 Geoffrey de Wirce held 8 hides in Feni Newbold, which most probably included Pailton, Stretton under Fosse, Easenhall. Yet in 1276 it is described as a member of Wappenbury, presumably as 5 knights fee of Roger de Mowbray by Thomas Wappenbury in 1166. Another Thomas later had 1 knights fee in Newbold apparently held of the king in Chief, in 1235 his estates passed to three sisters, Agnes was mother of Richard de Beyvill and conveyed her rights in 1261, Joan was mother of either Hugh Revel or, more probably to his wife Alice the descendants of the third sister, Margaret, who seem to have taken the name of Wappenbury.

The main manor of Feni Newbold, (it was given the name Fenny to identify it from the other Newbolds changed later to Fenny) it came to Hugh Revel, whose son had a grant of free warren in 1299, as did his son John in 1327. In 1316 William had made it over to John in tail, with a contingent remainder to his brother Robert of his estate here, consisting of 16 messuages, 11 virgates of land, with woodland meadow and pasture, and a mill, that somehow is recorded in all three places, Newbold, Pailton, Easenhall.

This John was knighted in 1351, as a knight of the shire, his son died leaving no issue, The deed name changed and became the **Manor of Newbold Revel** it was assigned to Alice, who married Sir John Malory of Winwick, Northants. In 1391, Sir John and Alice settled the Manor on themselves in tail. It descended in line to Sir Thomas Malory, whose widow died in 1480, the holding of it went to Richard, Duke of York, in right of his wife Anne, a representative of the Mowbrays.

It then passed to Sir Thomas's grandson Nicholas, aged 13. It was held in trust until he came of age when Nicholas Malory died in 1513, previously he had settled the reversion of the Manor, which he had held of Sir Maurice Berkley, who settled it on his elder daughter Dorothy and her husband Edward Cave.

It seems to have been divided up between the two daughters of Nicholas and so Margery, the younger with her second husband John Cope in 1557 who sold their share to Thomas Pope, He sold it to Sir William Whorwood, Solicitor- General who also bought the share from the other daughter Dorothy from her second husband George Ashby.

William Whorwoods daughter Margaret married Thomas Throckmorton, and they sold the manor in 1593 to Robert Stanford. His son, Charles left it to Elizabeth Aldersfoot in 1608, his widow. Now her son by a previous husband, Edward Morgan, is said to have sold it to Sir Simon Clarke, whose widow conveyed it to Sir Fulwar Skipwith, who had married her niece, his grandson Sir Fulwar built the existing mansion it continued with alterations and additions in the Skipwith hands until 1862.

The estate was left to Sir Thomas George Skipwith who immediately sold it to Edward Wood of Inverness!. The Woods made a good many alterations to the house and grounds in 1898, when Arthur Herbert Wood sold it to Col. Arthur Howard Heath, his son on whose death in 1911, sold it to Leopold Bernhard Bonn.

It was from his son Major Edward Bonn it was bought in 1931 by The British Advent Missions, Ltd of Watford, then in 1946 it was then, acquired by Sisters of Charity of St Paul as a training College for teachers.

It is now used as H.M. Prison Officers Training College.

Harborough Magna

Herdeberghhyrig

There is an early indication between 3-500bc of an ancient tribe called the Coritani who had dwellings in this area. The nearest trace is at Easenhall, and also of the Romano British settlers of up to the time that the Romans left in 410 ad. King Alfred in 878 ad. after the battle of Wedmore, re-established the Mercia kingdom.

The dividing line of the Roman Watling Street brought peace to the area, and a signal line of invasion was established from High Cross to Brinklow, on to Chesterton and so on down the Fosse way. Dwellings were warned with smoke by day and fire by night of marauders on the road. The area between the villages in the triangulation of the two Roman roads, (see map) became very prosperous, and many sought after this and other areas like Bromelaw, (Brinklow) Monks Kirby, Cestersover, Churchover Willey. Herdeberghyrig were also in great demand to build the amount of land each lord wanted to increase size of ownership and improve their standing.

At the time of the Domesday Book 1086, the two villages large and small were as one and called, Herdeburgehyrig.

Great speculation came over the valuation of this area.

Harborough Parva, and Harborough Magna,

Later at the time of the division once again they became one united for civil purposes, and called Harborough Magna.

Manors

Domesday Book records, it had 8 and a half hides, 4 and a half by Richard the Forester had this and 4 by Anseis in each case directly from the King . Richards holding had before 1066 been held by four Thegns freely, that of Anseis by Bruning. Hugh De Loges quitclaimed it to Roger de Herdebergh, in 1232 as Overlord, he was exempted from Assizes, Juries, and being made Sheriff, Verderer, or Coroner. By this time it had come into the hands of the Hastings family.

Henry de Hastings took over lordship, and Hugh, the son of Roger, held it by half a Knights fee, in 1269 assigned it to Joan, (Hastings widow) accepted it in Dower. Juliana le Blount widow of the second lord Hastings was granted this in a half fee, at £15 yearly, in dower 1325. In 1376 it was a very rewarding, and much sought after valuable Manor. Held by John de Hastings,who became Earl of Pembroke held Harborough in 1375 and Joan his widow assigned it to Sir William Beauchamp in 1431, This section remained in the family until when, in 1602 it was in the possession of Lord Grey of Ruthin. He was a member of the Hastings family.

The other manor was owned by Richard de Herdeburgh son of Hugh, died in 1284, leaving it to two daughters, as co-heiresses. Ela wife successively of Walter de Hopton and William de Boteler, the other daughter was Isabel wife of John de Hulles. In 1305 Ela after the death of her first husband, granted her half of the manor to her sister and brother in law, to hold from the chief lords John de Peyto, husband of Alice, daughter and heiress of John and Isabel, and previously wife of John de Langlye, settled the manor on his son John de Watervill in 1326, who held this as a moiety for life, he was brother in law to Alice de Peyto. In 1339 John de Peyto, the elder, granted the reversion of the manor after the death of John de Peyto the Younger, to Sir Walter de Hopton and Joan his wife.

The younger son John who was involved had a dispute in a lawsuit with the Abbott of Combe Abbey over waste committed in Harborough Magna in 1370. He then died in 1373 when the reversion came to John de Hopton, Sir Walter's son. The Hoptons continued to hold for some time as a full share, and sometimes as a moiety until the death of Walter Hopton in 1461, when it passed to the Corbet family of Moreton Corbet(Salop) this was by the marriage of his sister Elizabeth to Roger Corbet. His great, great grandson another Roger who died in 1538,settled the manor on Jerome and Robert, two of his younger sons, who with Roberts wife Jane passed it in 1569 to their eldest brother Sir Andrew Corbet, Robert the son of Andrew, died in 1583 and left two daughters as co-heiresses, Elizabeth who married Sir Hugh Wallop of Fairleigh (Hants) and Anne who had married Adolphus Cary of Berkhampstead (Herts) the latter and her husband conveyed their share to Oliver, Lord St. John of Blitsoe, and Roland Lytton in 1601 for settlement on Adolphus and Anne and her heirs, She died in 1602 and he in 1609, when it passed to her sister Elizabeth. In 1610 Sir Henry and Elizabeth Wallop conveyed the manor to Edward Riplingham. Alice his wife, and their son William. The last named dealt with his half of the manor to pay a fine in 1622. His estates were divided between his four daughters as co-heiresses, Harborough falling to Elizabeth Riplingham she died unmarried and bequeathed her half of the manor to Adolphus Oughton, the son of her eldest sister Anne. His grand son, Sir Adolphus Oughton, bart, was lord in 1710, he died 6 years later without legitimate issue. His widow Elizabeth was lady of the manor in 1740, after which time it changed hands several times.

In 1806 it was acquired by Sir Grey Skipwith, bart., and Harriet Townsend (his wife) remained so until he died in 1852. At this point trace is lost until 1900 when it was in the hands of the Boughton Leigh family. By 1936 the land was in the hands of Farmers, the Manorial rights have lapsed.

Yet another portion of the manor dating back to 1086 reads,

A priest is mentioned with four hides in 1086, so a portion of this may be a place of worship, and was granted in the reign of K.Henry III ;1327-1377 to Combe Abbey (the country was in the hands of Queen Isabella and her lover Mortimer).

Hasculph, son of Ankteil, de Herdebergh about 1327 was lord of the manor, and gave to Geoffrey de Langley, his chief messuage and all his land in Harborough, to hold of Sir Gilbert de Segrave, to which his daughter Isabel in 1257 added a messuage and a virgate of land which her father had given her. Hasculph seems to have left 3 daughters, Alice, Isoult (possibly Isobel) and

Maud the wife of John de Langlye , this is mixed up here since in 1255 the estate was given to the Monks at Combe! With an Advowson of the church given a rent of £10.61d a year reserved to the Langleys.

These rents and transactions came under controversy among the Langleys and related families finally being settled by John de Langleye and Ela his wife and also to Geoffery and his wife in 1325, five years later Geoffery died, Ela took a second husband William de Careswell, and her son Geoffery and his heirs for life

It passed through many hands from hereon, for in 1366 to Sir John Trillowe, then Baldwin de Fryvill in 1372, onto Sir Hugh Willoughby in 1452, when the estates were partitioned yet again. Thomas Ferrers 1459, his estates were seized by the Duke of Norfolk, who it was supposed represented the Segrave interests. Then the King became involved and it came into his possession in 1498 and worth 45s 8d. Sir John Ferrers had it in 1512 and left it to his uncle Roger Ferrers for life. Conveyed to John and Robert Cleaver in 1572, and in 1608 it was worth £7.01d.

The Abbot of Combe was holding a court in Harborough as early as 1258 and the grants made by the Langleyes were augmented by 12 acres and a third of a messuage from William de Venur and his wife Alice in 1279, had licence to alieniate land in mortain to this abbey, totalling at least 89 acres with 2 messuages, were granted in 1280, 1290, 1291, 1299. In 1539 at the dissolution the Combe abbey property in Harborough came into the hands of Mary Duchess of Richmond and Somerset.

The other lands in Axholme Lincs were granted to Thomas Mannyng, ex prior of Butley suffolk

It is also recorded whilst in the ownership of the De Langeleye family the manor was given in advowson to Combe Abbey. Ensuring the retention of rents of £10 6s a year by the family.

A great deal of changes went on with the ownership having rents worth £46 4s! The Duke of Norfolk had it with Sir Thomas Ferrers. The dates and owners of this profitable manor contradict the records, for example having given it to Combe Abbey, in 1482 John and Elizabeth Viellis, granted certain lands to the Carthusian Priory of Axholme Lincs. Although having previously said at the dissolution it was given to the Duchess of Richmond, it now says that it was granted to Thomas Mannying ex Prior of Butler Suffolk, and Bishop of Ipswich.

All Saints

The records show that the cultivation was measured in Hides(hides of a sheep cut into lengths and laid out as a strip, and measured in quantities to equate to 50-80 strips equalled a hide) and a villien or villager, would have his own plough. A bordar worked the land, and had an area at the top of a field (where the oxen turned at the border) for his own use. Although not slaves they would be sold with the land, and were not allowed to leave, or change masters. Life here was controlled by the Lord of the manor.

Ridge and Furrow farming running east to west, gave best results, and facing south a great asset. There was free ground for the workers to let their animals feed, Geese. Swine, Poultry all could run free and so allow them to provide for their families.

But not all manorial systems ran as freely as this, the Bailiff could take anything for the Lords table at will, in some cases bringing near starvation to the losers!

Housing for the most was of a stone base to roof where available and otherwise a basic wooden structure, supported by crutch and tie beams, purlins to hold the frame, laths for the roof of straw, wattle and daub infill, a centre hearth and a hole in the roof to let out smoke, a dirt floor (hence Dirt Poor) bedding and food was supported on shelves on posts. In winter the animals were brought in for safety and provide warmth. Dung stored and dried, they gathered furze, twigs, anything dried was used for fires.

This meagre type of cottage can still be seen today in many places around Britain, but with structural additions to roofing and windows and sanitation, timber framing a good indication by the wide spacing, close studding (uprights) indicated that this house could afford more timber and increased their security as well as stability and comfort. As wood became too expensive as well as restricted. Then came the Dutch influence they brought in the lump brick infill method, the design was known as Flemish Bond this style is still carried out in some building projects today, it improved the durability and reduced the incidence of fire and began a period of more enjoyable dwellings.

The Church

Although there is a record of a payment to a priest here with land in King Henry 111's time, it must have been a chapel but no foundations exist.

There is no record of a church earlier than the 14th century, to which date the Tower and north aisle and north and south arcades belong. In the 19th century, the Chancel and north and south isles were completely rebuilt. A Vestry and a clearstory also added. Walls redressed and a west doorway added.

The Chancel has been rebuilt with limestone and coloured limestone dressing.

The only window in the East wall has one of three trefoiled lights with a hood mould. The rebuilt south aisle has similar walling to the chancel. The vestry is a continuation of the aisle and has a square two sided window on the south, also one on the east, where there is a pointed doorway. The north aisle is built of limestone and red sandstone with a plinth and diagonal buttresses, the roof as are the others are steep pitched and tiled. It is light by a pointed moulded traceried window with three lights, with the exception of a few stones all has been renewed. On the west by a restored pointed traceried window with two trefoiled lights. Upper gabled walls have been rebuilt. Going towards the western end there is a blocked doorway with the remains if a floriated finial.

The Tower rises in three stages. Built of ashlar sandstone moulded plinth and a battlemented parapet, terminating with a pyramid roof and a weather vane. Western angles all rise in five stages worn by time, and carved grotesque heads. The lower stage refaced when the 16th century doorway was added, above the door there is a modern window with three cinquefoiled lights. In the next stage is the delight of the county, shows the time in the quarters by the symbols of the four evangelists, and Roman numerals to follow, bringing the story for all time of our Lord. The old wooden clock too difficult to wind had to be replaced and so this was the replacement, I could not find whose idea it was to adapt the figures, but A Mr. B. Poulston designed it in 1984. The old mechanism has been cleaned and stands in the porch for all the mechanical minded to gaze upon the workmanship of days gone by.

The belfry windows are on all faces and have two trefolied lights, with two gargoyles on north and south. The modern chancel has a tiled floor and one step to the Altar a pointed arch leads to the vestry. The Nave has a low pitched roof, thoughtfully reusing 17th c. trusses which have a pendant in the tie beams.

The clearstory arcades date from the 14th century and has two lights, sitting on octagonal pillars with richly carved bases.

The chancel arch is pointed and two splays resting on 19th c. responds, across the entrance is an oak screen, dated 1905, the pulpit and stone font are modern.

The south aisle at its eastern end has a traceried screen that leads into the vestry.

This is dedicated to children.

The north aisle has a trussed roof most probably of the same age as the clearstory, built in to the wall there is a richly moulded pointed arch with a misplaced finial which may have terminated in an Easter sepulchre. Giving a feeling of going nowhere, no doubt removed when the wall was rebuilt. This aisle commemorates the fallen and is the military chapel.

The Tower has a narrow doorway in the southwest angle splayed to take the staircase. On the wall is a painted list of 18th c. benefactions.

There are three bells recorded, that have a story all their own, the first in 1552,when the second book of common prayer was published, another in 1659 to commemorate the abdication of Richard Cromwell, made by Brian Eldridge, another in 1851 no doubt in line with the opening of the great exhibition in May that year, made by Mr. J.Taylor & son. The story runs that these bells could only be struck by hammers, on ropes, the Verger taking one rope in each hand and the third rope attached to his foot.

He would be bale to play several tunes, no doubt a fit man. There is a list of 43 incumbents in the nave, notable of these were, Rev, H. Holyoake of Rugby School, Rev. J. Lightfoot, Rev, Andrew Bloxam, Botanist and Historian.

ADVOWSONS The high regard for the value of Harborough Magna is shown in the long lists of advowsons made here. Presentations start from 1305 John de Langelye, his daughter in law 1330, again in 1336, then revoked on 1338, was then only made because a fine was imposed by Sir John Trillowe. Then moves on by dates Frevill Ferrers 1417, Adam Pershale 1577,William Boughton 1692, Theo Leigh 1780, since 1805 the advowsons have been in the hands of the Boughton-Leigh family.

There was a cottage called the Town House whose rents were allotted to pay for the lights in the church in 1563, by a tenancy to Anglionby of Balsall , and Henry Higsforde of Solihull.

Electricity was installed in 1932. Thus saving the tiresome job of lighting and changing the candles.

There are some interesting CHARITIES, from 1751 to distribute to the poor on Easter Monday and the rent from an estate in Long Lawford for roof repairs, both by Robert Scotton.

Earlier 1705 Gilbert Thacker gave the rents from a piece of land called little Mossel, for the apprenticeships of the parish.

Anne Blake willed in 1724, £5 from her estate in Churchover to be paid to the Minister, and also church wardens, and overseers to give to the poor, and is still awarded to those who assist in the running of the church.

Holyoaks Gift. It was recorded on a tablet that £5 being one years payment of Anne Blakes charity, not having been distributed the Rev. Mr. Holyoak gave £5 more, to be given to the poor In the parliamentary reports of that time that the Parish officers built a house on the land devised by Gilbert Thacker with the missing £5. Also another £5 given by the Rev. Thacker, and also £10 given by Robert Scotton, so that in respect of this, the rent of £20 and 20s is paid to the churchwardens for distribution with Anne Blakes charity to the poor. The charity commission dated 1861 appointed a body to distribute this money amounting to £60.0

Monks Kirby (Kirby)

The Priory is no longer there, but the magnificent rebuilt church remains.

The first church was founded in 917 by Ethelfleda daughter of King Alfred the Great. Later in 1077, it was given to a priest called Frano, together with furnishings to the Abbot of St Nicholas of Angers France, as well as 20 acres of corn land and the vill of Copston. In 1086 they had 2 ploughs teams 22 villiens, 6 Bordars and 6 ploughs all in 15 hides. This would have been very profitable.

The Domesday story.

In Saxon times it was a very important estate and owned by Leofwine. In the Domesday book it reads; Kirby has 15 hides, land for 20 ploughs. In lordship 6 male and 2 female slaves; 41 villagers and 2 smallholders with 2 priests who have 21 ploughs, meadow, 40 acres. In this manor two ploughs and 22 villagers and 6 smallholders with 5 ploughs. The total value was 100s, later 40s; now £10. Leofwin held it freely.

King William Rufus 3rd, 1090 gave vast areas of land to the Breton Knight, Geoffrey de la Guerche, (probably through his marriage to Alveva (Aelfgifu) which included large areas of land. Geoffrey rebuilt the ruined Saxon church, and dedicated it to the Blessed Virgin Mary, and St. Denis the patron Saint of France, in July 1077. He also endowed it with a Priory at Kirby and together with a priest called Frano, and also granted them the reversion of all that the priest called Frano held for him on his death

or cession. This followed with 20 acres of corn land, and the ville of Copston. In 1086 the monks of St Nicholas are recorded as having 2 plough teams, 22 villiens, and 6 bordars with 5 ploughs of Kirby manor, which was rated as 15 hides!

On the death of Geoffrey de la Guerche, (a carved stone head can still be seen, and is said to be that of Geoffery) King Henry V granted the lands to Neil de Aubigny, who had a son called Roger de Mowbray who confirmed and increased the lands where the monks of the abbey established an alien priory and named it MONKS KIRBY.

In 1242 three quarters of a fee in Kirby was held by the prior for Roger de Mowbray which included 4 carucates of land, £4, a windmill 10s, and rents valued at £10 4s 10d, 4 carucates in Walton 80s and 3 in Copston worth only 30s all this and other fees loaned to the church made them fairly comfortable, and allowed great improvements of the monastery. There were other additions to their existence for in K. Henry 111's. Time, 1266 he allowed the monks a fair at midsummer and a market in Kirby on Wednesday. In 1305 this was a bit inconvenient and a special dispensation was given for Tuesday. Maybe it was because they were given free warren in Kirby, Walton , Paylington also they were given view of frankpledge for their tenants in Kirby, Cestersover, Walton, Little Newnham and elsewhere so that they could pay the exchequer 5 marks yearly until 1412 when it was assigned to Richard Boomer, keeper of the Pantry. All this good living came to an end when the wars with France started, and since this was an alien priory of Angers it was seized into the kings hands, and Sir Canon Robsart became his holder of the lease for 25 years on rental of £40 annually from the monks of Axholme Priory.

He died before the lease ran out so his son John took over, shortly after that Thomas Mowbray, Duke of Norfolk arranged for the transference to his favourite abbey of Carthusians at the Isle of Axholme, so that by 1535 they were receiving a large sum of £96 0s 10d! The dissolution brought much needed wealth to Thomas Mannyng Bishop of Ipswich, who was also Master of the college of Mettingham (Suffolk). Charles Brandon Duke of Suffolk bargained for the transfer on the dissolution assignments, Henry Grey Duke of Suffolk died in 1559 it passed to his daughter

Katherine, married to Edward Seymour, Earl of Hertford. Their grandson William sold the manor to Mary, countess of Buckingham, who settled it on her grandson Basil, Lord Fielding, created Earl of Denbigh in 1622, in whose family it has Descended.

Saint Edith's.

The Church

It consists of a chancel, nave, north and south aisles and chapels, south porch, vestry, and a tower built into the south west corner. The church had suffered much in the past, and amends began in the 14th century, again in the 15th century when the present arcades were built, upper part of the tower rebuilt, and most of the windows replaced. The priory buildings on the north side were built in the church during the rebuilding in 15th century. Apart from the blocked openings of a door jamb offset for upper floor in the chapel and a line of a steep roof on the wall in the chancel, nothing remains of the old chancel building.

Re- roofed about the end of the 16th c. it was re roofed again in the 17th c. re-leaded and has an inscription dated 1709 according

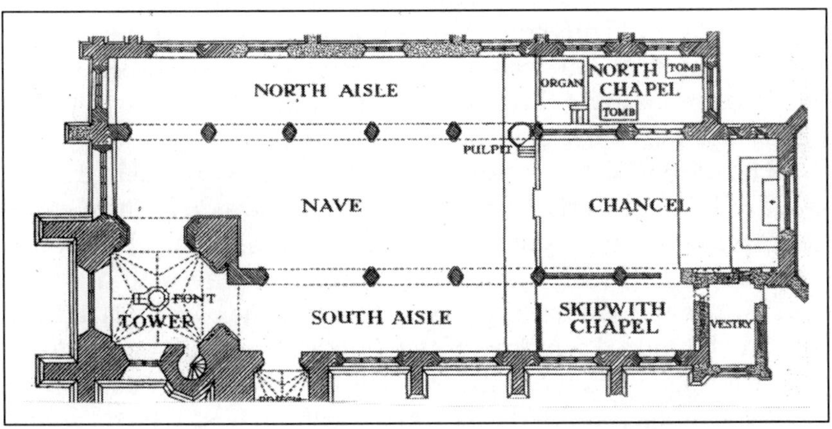

Plan of Saint Edith's.

to a piece saved in the 19th c. and was shown fixed on the east wall, of the parvise.

The general arrangement of the church layout is rather unusual, until recent times the nave extended into the chancel without an arch. The church has a lofty appearance and has no clearstory, with the windows placed at a rather high position from the floor. The tower is tall and exceptionally large, originally it had spire, but this was blown down on Christmas night 1722.

Most of the east wall has been refaced, and a three trefoiled light is modern. The lower part of the north wall is of ashlar, in which there is an umbry, with an opening also with a four centered head, both blocked with masonry. The upper part of alternate courses of ashlar and rubble has a line of a steep pitched roof with a blocked splayed opening below. On the south a low modern vestry replaces a small earlier one. It has a pointed doorway, a two light square headed-window on the east and another on the south, diagonal buttress at the angle, and a low buttress against the aisle wall, terminates in a crocketed finial. The roof is a low pitched lean-to one with a plain parapet. Above the vestry the wall has been largely refaced and has a 16th century window inserted into a hollow square-headed recess; it is of three cinquefoiled lights with a transom under a four-centred head. The east wall of the south aisle above the vestry is lighted by a traceried window of three cinquefoil lights, under a head with a hood mould. The south wall, which has a moulded plinth, is divided into four bays by buttresses, each in two stages terminating in pinnacles with crocketed finials above a plain parapet. At sill level there is a weathered offset, around a string course. The east bay has a pointed traceried window of two lights, the remaining three have wide windows of three trefoiled lights, and the centre ogee and the others pointed.

The Porch is two- storied, built of sandstone ashlar. The gable, which formerly contained a sundial, was rebuilt in stone of classic mid 19th century, omitting the sundial. The south entrance is of a richly moulded pointed archway, with a string course over as hood mould. Above this arch the parvise is lighted by a small pointed window of two lights, and on the east side by a narrow ogee-headed window. The ground floor has a stone vaulted ceiling, moulded ribs. Carved central boss. The doorway has an elaborately pointed arch of three orders and all three have moulded bases. The wall of the north aisle, with the exception of a portion of the west bay, was rebuilt in the 10th century copies of the previous ones. It is lighted by four traceried windows of three trefoiled lights in deep hollowed splays under four centred heads; the one at the west end the east jamb are original. At the west end there is a small added buttress, close to the original one, which has a moulded string course and gabled head. The chapel at the eastern end is divided in two bays by a rebuilt buttress. Both bays have a traceried window of three lights under a four-centred head in deep splays. Below there is a splayed offset for a floor of the destroyed Priory buildings. The east wall is again of stone mixture, continues at the north end as a buttress and contains the south jamb of a doorway. It has a restored three-lighted window. A large modern buttress divides this wall from the west end of the nave, which has a large pointed window of four lights, in a hollow splay. The tracery is modern.

The lower half of the tower, which has a moulded plinth, is of ashlar. The rebuilt is of lighter ashlar. It rises in three stages, with buttress in five weathered stages at the angles of the south and west walls, and terminates in 19th century parapet with open trefoil- headed panels, central pediments, crocketed headed pinnacles with weather vanes at each angle. On the west side the ground floor is lighted by a tall pointed three-light traceried window, of three orders, and on the south by a similar window, but of two trefoiled lights with restored tracery. The second stage has traceried windows of two trefoiled lights with transoms under four centered heads and hood moulds, on east, south and west. The belfry windows on each face are similar, but with a string-course at sill level. On the east side above the ringing- chamber window there is a clock dial. Against the buttress at the south east angle the wall is splayed out for the tower staircase, which is lighted by six loop-lights, three ogee headed in the lower stages and three round headed in the rebuilt portion.

The Chancel has a tiled floor with three steps to the altar placed against a carved stone reredos with a central cross of alabaster. The walls of the eastern end are of rough coursed rubble and then of red sand stone; two bays of the south arcade and one of the north are included in the chancel by a dwarf wall of light coloured ashlar and oak screens. The dwarf wall extends across and to embrace the chapels. At the eastern end of the south wall there is a trefoil-headed piscine under a pointed arch on attached shafts with moulded capitals and bases, and a triple sedilia with pointed arches, the inner supported on circular shafts with moulded capitals and bases. Between them is a narrow blocked doorway with a four -centred arch with spandrels. All this portion of the wall has been rebuilt of light ashlar, the sedilia and piscine are restorations. The door way is original. High up there is a narrow rectangular opening on the same level is a narrow trefoil opening into the chapel. Below is a modern unglazed four light window and west of it the east bay of the arcade, closed by a dwarf wall and oak screen.

Hung on the north wall is a framed painted portrait royal arms of Charles 11 dated 1660. The south side takes two bays of the arcade, the east one partly blocked by a modern wall buttress, Both bays are closed by walls and oak screens, with an opening into the chapel.

The South Chapel, known as the Skipwith Chapel, has a hatchment on the south wall bearing the Skipwith coat of arms. Part of the east wall was rebuilt in ashlar, with an ogee headed doorway, and a hood-mould when they added the vestry. At the southern end of this wall is a moulded ogee trefoil-headed piscine, the projection cutaway and above it a moulded carved bracket. Built into the wall on north side of the east window there is a small square panel with a carved shield of arms.

The east window has a moulded four centred-rear; the south window has splayed jambs with a pointed arch.

The North Chapel is stone paved for 20 feet, and six steps above the level of the nave, the remainder being occupied by the organ. In the angles of the east wall there are niches with mutilated canopies of ogee trefoils, pilasters, with crocketed finials, and battlemented bracket pedestals. To the west of the narrow light to the chancel there are traces of a destroyed dividing wall.

Here there are two large white alabaster tombs of similar design, one in the north east corner to Sir William Fielding, died 1547, and Elizabeth his wife, died 1539, with their life sized effigies; William is in armour with a book clasped in his conjoined hands, clean shaven, wearing three rings on each hand and is without a ruffle, Elizabeth is also clasping a book wearing a ruffle, and with three rings on each hand. This book indicates the replacement of Latin in the church services with English. This was also the year that the marriage ring changed hands, and the rings could signify the marriage rings. The pedestal is divided into five panels, three with shields coats of arms, at the end into two, both with shields. The other tomb is of Basil Fielding, son of William, date of death left blank, and Gooddeth his wife, died in 1580. The two effigies are similar to the others but Basil has a beard, and wears a ruffle, his feet rest on a lion and his gauntlets rest beside his right leg, each clasping a book, each wearing two rings on each of both hands. On the hem of Gooddeth's dress there are two small sleeping dogs, one on either side. At the east end of the pedestal are two shields, at the other a shield supported by undraped figures, showing the family motto. On the south side there are three shields, each held by a woman, and three infants in winding sheets; and on the opposite side three shields, one supported by a man and woman and two held by men, one dressed in armour the other a civilian, and a woman with her hands clasped in prayer with two infants in winding sheets. Somewhere there is an explanation of the stories behind all this and would make fascinating reading.

Fielding Family tombs.

The Nave is of red sandstone ashlar walls and modern floor tiles. The north arcade consists of six bays and the south has five of moulded pointed arches that die out on plain tall lozenge shaped pillars with moulded bases. Two bays of the south arcade one of the north extend into the chancel due to the presence of the tower. At the west end the wall has been increased in thickness with modern light ashlar; the window has a hollow pointed arch. The tower arch is richly moulded dying out to half hexagonal responds. On the east wall of the tower as it projects into the nave, it is visible to see the roof line of the earlier structure. Hung on the west wall there is a plan of the seating with the names of the occupiers, dated 1752. The pulpit on the north side is a modern one of stone is placed on the north side of the chapel.

The lectern is in magnificent brass and a delight to the eye.

The north isle has three blocked doorways with four centred heads at the east end, two on the ground floor and above one on floor. Built into the north wall is a badly mutilated head, (as stated earlier) which I am told is the head of the man who rebuilt and dedicated it in 1077, Geoffrey de la Guerche (or Wirce). Against the north wall at the west end there are two white marble monuments, of similar design to the 7th Earl of Denbigh, he died 1865, and his wife died 1847; the other is a to Lady Augusta Fielding died 1848. There are three small tablets to other members of the family. Also the west wall has been thickened here similar to the nave. The South Aisle has a modern tiled floor the tower arch is richly moulded partly blocked to respond to the later arcade. The windows have two splayed arches continuing down to the sills, and the door appointed to the rear arch of two plain orders. Above the door is a small ogee light to the parvise.

The Tower has a modern tiled floor and a modern octagonal font in the centre. It has a stone vaulted ceiling moulded ribs and a central octagonal boss. In the south east angle there is an ogee headed doorway to a circular stairway leading to the tower and a parvise; above the door is a painted list of charities, dated 1714, both windows have deeply splayed arch to reveals. Round the walls is a dado of oak panelling cut from the old bell frame of 1921 when it was replaced by a steel one. The traceried screen enclosing the chapel and the chancel are also made from these timbers.

The Roof of the nave and aisles, which extend the whole length of the church date from the 16th century and were probably carried out by the Duke of Suffolk.

The nave roof is low pitched and is divided into 12 bays by trusses supported on brackets with traceried spandrels and moulded wall posts. The tie beams ridges purlins and wall plates, are moulded, some are battlemented. At the west end the truss, which is shortened by the tower, has solid instead of a traceried bracket.

Both aisle roofs are of the lean to type and of similar design. Over the south aisle it is divided into six bays by moulded beams resting on a moulded wall plate supported on stone corbels on the arcade wall. Each bay is divided by an intermediate beam and by two purlins, both moulded. Three bays at the end have carved bosses at the junction of the purlins with the intermediate beams. The north aisle has a roof of nine bays, but without the carved bosses. Some of the timbers of the western bays have been renewed probably 18th century, and much of the roof has been re boarded.

The Bells the oldest date from the 14th century; three by Henry Bagley, 1618, 1623, 1640; one by Joseph Smith, 1711, and one by Thomas Eayre of Kettering.

The Plate consists of a silver gilt flagon, chalice, ciborium, and paten, all are a gift of the Duchess of Dudley, 1638. There is also a silver chalice and cover of 1585; a silver paten inscribed I.H.S. and bearing a defaced crucifix .

The register commences in 1653.

CHARITIES.

Joseph Bosworth by will dated 20 December 1805 gave £63, to have interest payment of £42 to be paid to the minister to preach a sermon on Mid-lent Sunday and the following Sunday, after St. Swithin, the interest of £21 for the Sunday school for the poor children of Monks Kirby and Pailton, if discontinued in either place,then to pay one half of the interest to the said minister o preach second Sunday after 29 September. The testator by a codicil dated 8th March 1806 left a close of land in Pailton called Shuckborough close to the vicar of Monks Kirby upon the trusts contained in his will, this annually amounts of £10.

Thomas Cook, a tablet placed in the church in 1714 states that he gave in his will arable land for the maintenance of the church, £1 5s 4d to be applied to the church wardens for church purposes. John King, who died in 1642, by will charged certain lands in Street Ashton lordship called Fat Furlong with the annual payment of 10s paid at Christmas, and at Easter, and at Whitsun tide to the poor of Monks Kirby town.

William Miller by will gave Gills Close near Pailton, ordering the rent to be distributed yearly among the poor of the Constable ward of Monks Kirby. Amounting to £8, together with the 10s, amount of John Kings Charity to be distributed among the widows and old people residing in the parish.

Lady Mary Frances Katherine Fielding, by her will in August 1895 bequeathed £3.000, the interest to be to be applied to all or any of the following purposes (a) towards the salary of the minister of the church of England who shall conduct divine service in the chapel of ease known as St. Denis at Pailton, (b) to towards the maintenance of the work of the church of England in the said parish (c) towards the maintenance of the Lady Mary's home in the parish so long as the purposes and uses of the home are continued in accordance with the principles of the church of England. Annual income amounts to £60, approximately.

Lady Mary Frances Catherine Fielding by her will dated August 1895 bequeathed £3,000 for the following purposes, (a) towards paying for the salary of the minister of the church of England to divine service in the chapel of ease at St. Denis pailton, (b) towards the maintenance of any branch of the work of the church of England. (c) towards the maintenance of the Lady Mary's home in the parish so long as the purposes and uses of the home are continued in accordance with the principles of the church of England.

Lady Mary's Home. By an indenture 18 March 1880 Lady Mary Frances Katherine Fielding granted to the trustees of the property then known as Pailton Hall, upon trust for the benefit solely of the inhabitants of the parish of Monks Kirby, for the

instruction of the young and the care of the sick and aged being always among

The principal objects in view, subject to such regulations of the Archdeacon of Coventry, the vicar of Monks Kirby, or any trustees of the major part them should with the approval of the Bishop of the Diocese appoint. The following scheme for the management of the home; was approved by the Bishop of Worcester in the commencement of the year 1913.

'The net proceeds after paying legal fees and providing for the maintenance of the property, may be applied by the trustees at their discretion for any of the following objects:

A. the poor, (1) Gifts in time of sickness or any special necessity. (2) Obtaining admission to hospitals, convalescent homes or suchlike institutions, or providing special medical or surgical appliances.

B, Church schools contributions, which fall upon the managers of elementary schools.

C. Contributions for providing an extra clergyman in the parish, in consideration of his efficient care of the poor, the sick, and the aged, the amount not to exceed one quarter of the net revenue in any year.

The charity is regulated by the Charity Commissioners dated 20 December 1918 and directs that the yearly income be applied as directed by the Bishop in 1913, or any other charity as directed and approved by the Bishop.

Pailton

(Paylington)

Revel. Ermine a cheveron gules and a border engrailed sable.

The name is derived from the Anglo Saxon name of Paelle or Paegel (which implies a homestead).

There are indications that there were Norman settlers in 1070.

At the beginning of the 13th century the manor of Pailton was in the hands of William de Turville, who assented to his son William endowing his wife Maud (de Hastings) therein 1217, after the death of the younger William, Maud claimed the whole manor as a Dower, while her father in law would only grant one third of it. The younger William having died without issue, his estates were divided between his two sisters, Cecily wife of Roger de Craft, and Isabel, who married Walhamet le Poure, who also left no issue. However Roger de Crafts son, Roger was succeeded by his sisters, Isabel wife of Hugh de Herdeburgh and Beatrice, whose first husband was William de Chameless, accordingly in the list of knight's fees of Edmund, Earl of Lancaster. We find a half fee in Pailton and Harborough held by Nicholas de Turville and a quarter each held by Hugh de Herdebergh and George de Chameless in Pailton.

The Manors

William de Chameless, son of Sir Henry, of Bedworth was dealing with lands here between 1330 and 1345, and in 1405 the lands late of his son John, apparently the last of his line, were in the hands of trustees, as you would expect, this quarter fee cannot be traced or even where the money went.

Isabel. One grand daughter of Hugh de Herdebergh married John de Hullesand and had two daughters, Denise, married John de Waterville, and Alice married first John de Langley and then John Peyto. As they were under 30 years at the time of the his hand in the rebellion in 1322, their lands were held of him, since it was possessed of in the honour of Leicester, and were seized with the King's hands. (Rebellion of the Lords over Kings Henry VI's lover Roger Mortimer), but were restored in 1324. Denise left no issue, and in 1361 John de Payto, held a quarter-fee in Pailton , which was assigned to Maud, one daughter of Henry, Duke of Lancaster.

Ella sister of de Hulles, married Walter de Hopton and their descendant Walter died in 1461 seized of 4 messuages and 4 carucates of land in Pailton. Which then passed to his sister Elizabeth wife of Roger Corbet and so it descended, being sometimes styled a manor, with Great Harborough to the family hands of Oughton.

William Revel had a grant of free warren in his demesnes at Pailton in 1304, as did John Revel in 1327.

The pastures and the development of huge flocks of sheep brought wealth to the landowners, and helped to develop Coventry. Unfortunately the dissolution and the wool market began collapsing brought extreme hardship and poverty and discontent to this area.

This manor then descended with Newbold Revel until 1537,when John Cope and Marjory(Malory) his wife who sold their moiety to Thomas Pope. The other moiety was retained by Dorothy (Malory) and her husband Edward Cave and was held by her two daughters in 1545 and by the younger, Margaret wife of Thomas Boughton, at her death in 1565, when the manor was said to be the property of the Duchy of Lancaster.

Margaret was succeeded by her eldest son Edward Boughton. It was probably this manor of Pailton that was held by the Skipwiths from 1728 until about 1850, by this date the Earl of Denbigh was said to be Lord of this manor.

Pailton Story

It was after the dissolution of the monasteries in 1538, great hardship fell on the many areas, Paylington which was close by Monks Kirby and under its control were particularly affected, a recession of land values, the topography changed from pasture to rough ground. This caused much hardship for the villiens, bordars, and freemen, all were tied to the land as it came up for sale and change. Destitution was everywhere, with little or no consideration from the revised landowners. K. Henry VIII. gave the rights of Monks Kirby and all the lands in the area to Trinity College Cambridge, and huge tithes were exacted for their benefit. Putting the land under the plough did not bring immediate relief to the villagers, yet still the sub-let owners demanded greater returns to meet the tithes and provide for the owners, Trinity College. This brought resentment and bitter feelings. Strict practices were brought in by Trinity College. They selected a local to control the area.

Mr. Podmore, MA. A resident vicar, of Willey became their representative whose lust for power and greed for money, both for him and the college, exacting harsh returns on late and failed payments of tithes lead him to bring rough justice.

Without any one to fight their corner, starvation and extreme hardship meant that life hung on a thread or the whim of Podmore.

The populace were even refused the ancient right of collection by hook and by crook, in order to provide for cooking, heating etc. they had to go into the woods and forests to steal in order to survive; even small rodents and animals meant something for the children. Mr. Podmore's harsh treatment was strict, if they were caught with more than one pounds worth of herbage, they could be sentenced to the Colonies, whipped, imprisoned, and fined even heavier This brought about riots and Violent disorder.

Examples of the tithes;

Herbage tithe for cattle to pail and breed	£10	4s	10d
Herbage for sheep reared	£4	10s	0d
Bees, Ducks, Geese and Hens	£0	10s	0d
Horses	£2	0s	0d
600 Lambs	£46	7s	0d
Wool from 1211 shorn sheep	£53	6s	5d

This would be increased annually. This Mr. Podmore soon found life unbearable here at his residence in Pailton House, when the poverty, hard driven populace threw stones and bricks and even peppered his door with gunshot.

This Podmore extended his reign of terror to other villages also within the Trinity College arrangement of tithes, Withybrook, Willey, Copston Magna, Flecknoe, and Sawbridge. He even made the Earl of Denbigh give the money for his tithes.

He married a local girl much younger than himself, had two children, and deservedly suffered ill health and died in 1842, his wife Sarah followed him in 1850. They are buried at Willey.

However back to the story, In 1673 nine inhabitants petitioned Trinity College, that having held the land for a specified period of time, gave them right of ownership and requested that this freely held land should be free of tithes. After much consultation and being made aware of the civil unrest and to preserve the peace this was granted.

In 1771 the enclosure acts brought out the surveyors, regardless of forgoing arrangements with landowners and the workers of the land, they enclosed the land with Wattle and Quick Thorn of the two of the greatest pastures 127 acres. Gave a breakaway of five acres for the poor to grow vegetables and gather furze thereon. It still left the woods and all its financial advantage to Trinity College to enjoy.

By 1773 Trinity College made a settlement with 12 inhabitants, they condescended to grant for the good and peace of the area, so that no disruption or disquiet should prevail. They gave lists of those with free pasturage up to a small amount, for the well being of the populace, and that on Lady Day they should pay one couple of Capons, or two shillings and sixpence in money.

In 1883 the whole area was purchased by the Earl of Denbigh for a Fox Covert and a hunting area, with a game reserve. The amount of bad feeling created was unbelievable to the populace so this was a time to take matters into their own hands It all came to a head with court action, the defendants were acquitted.

The Earl of Denbigh is Lord of the Manor still.

The Church

Pailton church is outside the time factor of this article, It was Consecrated in 1904, suffice to say that it is of a delightful Romanesque design, the Architect was a Mr Cheiake from Hereford.

Pailton church.

The unusual selection of Red bricks interlaced with white stone, in Hollington Red and Campden yellow stone which at the Circular East end, gives a warm and pleasing welcome. To enter into this lovely church brings a warm sense of awe and delight at the spread of colour and the sweeping design of the Nave.

Obviously modern but what a refreshing change to get away from the Gothic and all other ancient designs so expected in churches, which were intended to overwhelm the feelings by such stylised grandeur. This is worthy of a visit to sweep away all the cobwebs.

This lovely warm pleasant church bears the dedication and love of the people of Pailton and the sacrifices they made to make it possible. It is a credit to the community.

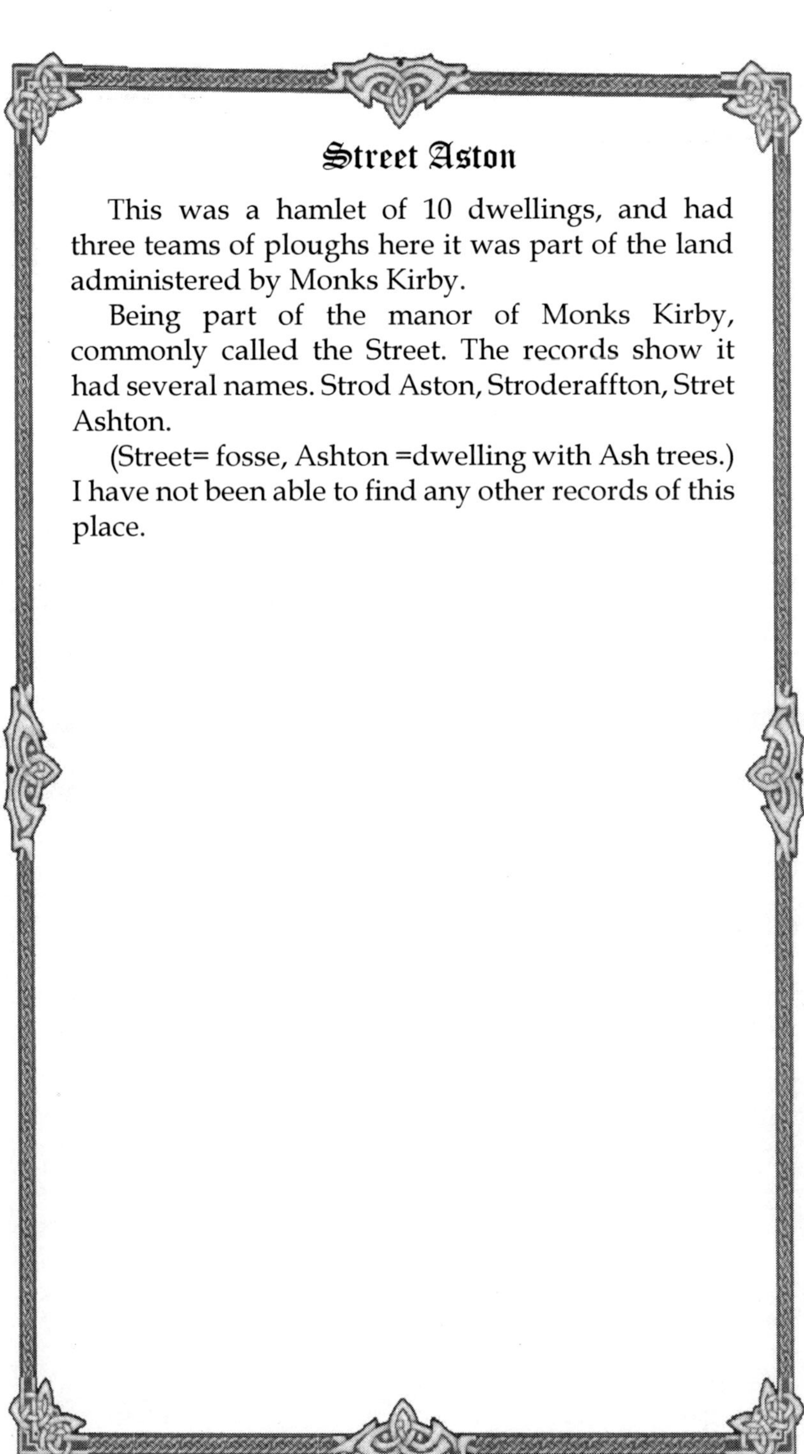

Street Aston

This was a hamlet of 10 dwellings, and had three teams of ploughs here it was part of the land administered by Monks Kirby.

Being part of the manor of Monks Kirby, commonly called the Street. The records show it had several names. Strod Aston, Stroderaffton, Stret Ashton.

(Street= fosse, Ashton =dwelling with Ash trees.) I have not been able to find any other records of this place.

Stretton under Fosse

Stroder Subtus Fosse

This was first mentioned in 1086 in a land deal with Newbold it included Pailton Easenhall, and again in a transfer of part of a 5 knights fee in 1166 between Roger de Mowbray and Thomas de Wappenbury part of Newbold Revel 1327. The family Revell, a descendant by a daughter and heir to Malory; and from that by marriage to the family Cave, then from that marriage, came the heir to family Andrews, and then passed to the Boughton family into NewboldRevel.

A Thomas Andrews Esq. levied a fine whereby it was found that Margaret Boughton (one of the daughters and co-heirs of Edwin Cave) had died and Thomas Andrews seized it, without true allegiance, he had thought he had the right since it had been left under aged, by Margaret Boughton to her son and heir, just 20 years of age.

Domesday book reads. Hereabouts it was said it had twenty houses and seven teams of ploughs.

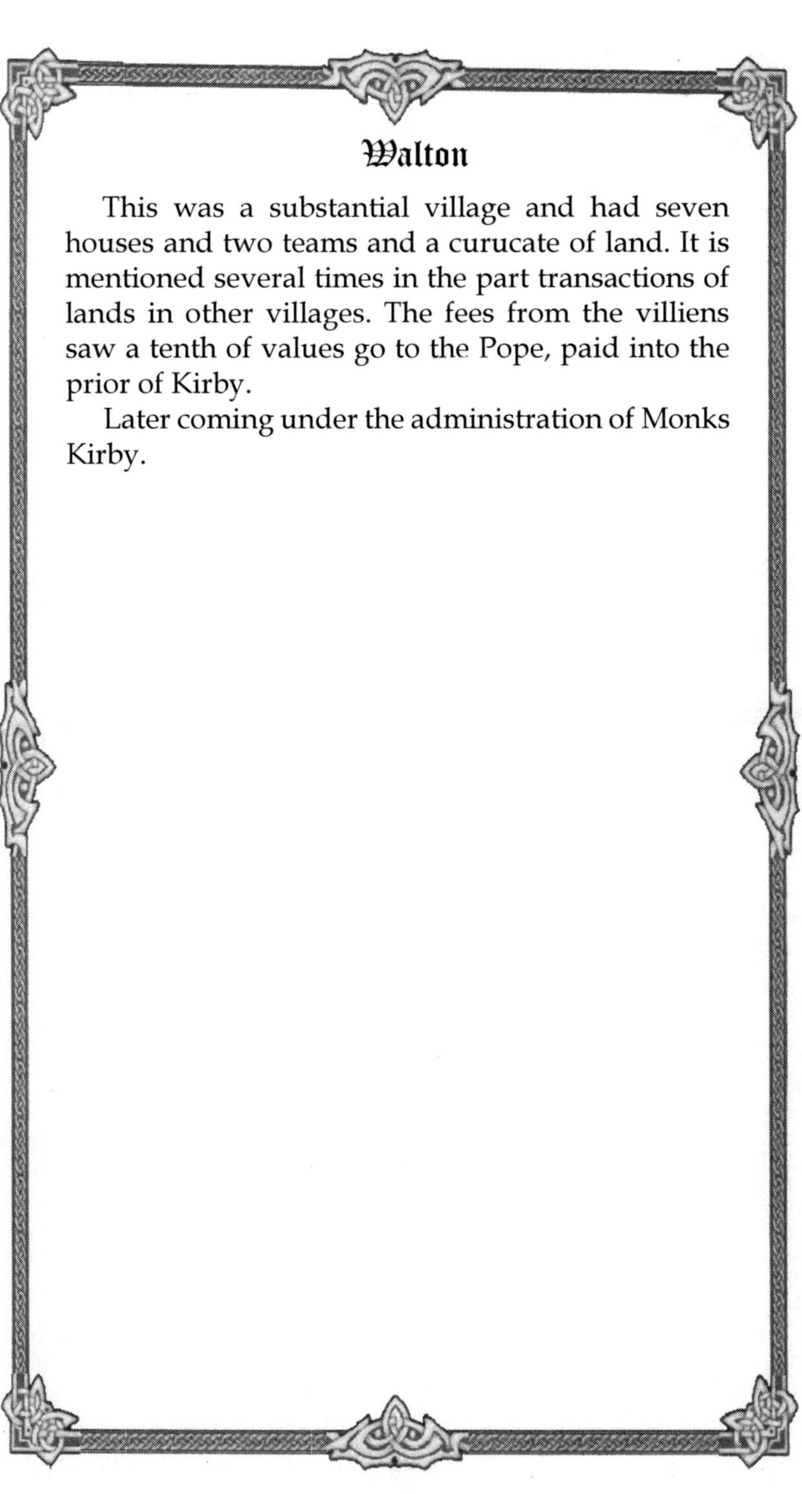

Walton

This was a substantial village and had seven houses and two teams and a curucate of land. It is mentioned several times in the part transactions of lands in other villages. The fees from the villiens saw a tenth of values go to the Pope, paid into the prior of Kirby.

Later coming under the administration of Monks Kirby.

Brockhurst

Have not found out much about this place except that it was mentioned as a knights fee, of Lord Mowbray, and much later, in the estates of the Earl of Denbigh. There is a lane that still identifies the village.(The village name comes from a bank by the stream, Bank is a 'Hurst', Stream is a 'Brock.').

Willey

(Wilega)

Willey is mentioned in the Domesday book together with Wibtoft and was then in lands with Count de Muelan.

The lands were quite substantial, so it was divided into Quarters. The whole movement of ownership briefly related here, it is outlined by primary dates, omitting much of the settlements by lawsuits, debts, and stories of successions.

The lands, which included Wibtoft, and Bedworth were prosperous. In 1180-1 it was in hand with Robert de Wilega, (after whom the village is named) who was owed two Marks by Simon de Verdun concerning lands here.

1197 William de Turvill owed £80 on his lands at Fulbrook and Willey, to Arron the Jew, In 1208 an intermediate tenancy was granted in that year also holding Bedworth and Willey as one fee. In 1309, in the reign of K. Henry VIth, Hugh de Herdebergh granted Willey to Nicholas de Herdebergh and his heirs. He received rents in Brailes and Willey. Nicholas died without issue in 1315 his surviving relatives, came from as far afield as Wem, Shropshire, Ela and Isabel, also John de Peyto came into ownership of the whole of Willey. This led to fines and a lawsuit regarding ownership, settlements were made placing it in two halves, one half laying to the east. This again was disputed in 1345 and came in to the hands of William de Botoler who was the right heir of his mother Ela. John de Peyto was still alive in 1345 when he did fealty to Edmund de Botelera fine having been concluded in which Ela granted the reversion of the manor to her second son. This brought trouble with a lawsuit between Ela, John and Alice, and William de Boteler, William stated that it was granted to him by Hugh de Herdeburgh in fee.

It was granted as being in tail legalising the grant of 1345.

(There are some strange movements of property from this point onwards)

Williams brother, a priest on whose death in 1376. Willey was let out into four parts, with exception of the Windmill producing a princely sum of £8 11s 4d, a court settlement made it into four part ownership. One part because Elizabeth was a minor, so it came in the hands of K. Edward 111. The following year Margaret and her husband Fulk dePenebrugg quitclaimed their quarter of the manor of Willey to Walter de Cokesey for 100 marks.

The strange share now passed to Ankeretta, who was Elizabeth's aunt in 1413 and to her son Gilbert before 1422 when it was yet again divided into thirds. One third of which was held in dower by Gilberts Widow Beatrice, the other two went into the Kings coffers again. Gilbert's child being under age of Ankaretta, to whom Sir John Talbot was Gilberts brother was heir and successor he was then created Earl of Shrewsbury in 1442, it remained in his family until the 7th Earl died in 1616 the Talbot estates were divided and the Willey estate came into the hands of Elizabeth the Countess of Kent, however she died in 1640 and left no heirs. Willey came into the hands of her brother in law Thomas Howard Duke of Norfolk in 1679 when it was reduced to one messuage of land and was used to pay off family debts.

Another quarter in the hands of Henry Leigh, whose son and successor sold it to several private persons in 1663. John Jorden, and Richard Garrett in 1640 , who had tenements at this time of which this was a part.

The other two quarters, one was bought by Sir Hugh de Cokesey in 1377, he died in possession in 1445 and it was settled to his wife in tail who died in 1460, who passed it to Joyce Beauchamp she died 1473 it was passed on to Sir John Grevyle, her son by a previous marriage Thomas Greville alias Cokesey, died in 1509, when license to enter was granted to distant cousins R. Russell and R. Winter family. It was then that this part of Willey

St. Leonard's church, Willey.

came into the hands of the Winter family by then descended into three generations. George great grandson of Robert sold the estates when he came of age in 1565 but peculiarly was still in his hands when he died in 1593 his son Robert was concerned in a recovery of debt in 1604. Later In 1694 manorial rights came into the hands of the Fielding family Earls of Denbigh, Newnham Paddox who were lords in 1830, where Court Leets were held.

Church

Saint Leonard

It is thought that the Nave and Tower may date from the late 14th century- early 15th.

It has undergone extensive modern restoration.

Chancel was rebuilt, and enlarged with a Vestry on the north side.

A deep south porch was added at the same time, where were mediaeval services began by conducting baptisms, churching of women, also marriage services, then proceeded into the church with great ceremony.

South side wall was refaced parapets added to the nave and a stair turret. The west was resurfaced with ashlar.

Chancel is of red sandstone and rubble with light coloured stone dressings.

Chancel on the south being well light with cinquefoil and traceried windows with a trefoil headed doorway between. The Vestry is of the same material and is roofed with slates, it has two-light windows on the north and is entered from the west

The north side is of red sandstone and ashlar, lighted with a square headed window of three cinquefoil lights.

The door on the north side is blocked up, as many churches are upon an old superstition that it was here where the Devil dwelt it was blocked so as not to bring him with you to worship, (at one time before being blocked, a child coming here for christening was brought in this door, and when christened left by the west door leaving the devil behind!) here you can see an outline of the door and below is a beautiful mock tomb recess with a figure of a person with hands clasped in prayer, one wonders about the story behind this and how it came about and who was the person depicted? Part of the restoration project after the fire in 1678.

On this wall holds a hidden story of a rare medieval distemper painting, arranged in panels and has a dado, this has been painted over. Coventry's Parish church had the opportunity to restore their painting of Doom could this happen to Willey?

Probably not, since there is so much to be done elsewhere in the church.

At the angle is a small modern buttress there is a 19th century battlement with lions headed gargoyles. At the west end there is a half octagon staircase.

The south side completely refaced with two windows, and a pointed entranceway. With rebuilt buttresses, a parapet battlement is repeated, there is a projecting half octagonal stair turret built of rubble dressing with a loop light and a battlemented parapet probably 19th century. The south side completely refaced is lighted with two windows to match the other side, buttresses at each end, one in the centre, this is repeated on the south side. Between them is a porch built of small rubble similar to the chancel. It has a single small light. The entrance has a pointed arch of two splays.

There are buttresses at each end and one in the centre, all three inbuilt. The battlemented parapet on the north is repeated. The Chancel arch is pointed with two splayed orders, on half-octagon responds with moulded capitals and bases; the tower arch is also pointed. These die out on the walls unlike the roof the orders are 16th century and has three bays with wall trusses at each end and are supported on curved brackets and wall posts. The beams, purloins and wall plates are richly moulded and in the centre of each tie beam there is a carved boss; some of the purlins, and rafters have been replaced

THE TOWER

Built of sandstone ashlar, is six foot square with moulded plinth with parapet, rises in three stages. Diminished by weathered offsets. At the western angles there are diagonal buttresses rising in six stages, the upper stages forming bases for pinnacles now missing; at the eastern angles the buttresses are at right angles to both north and south walls. It has windows of two trefoiled lights under a four-centered head, a quatrfolied light in the ringing chamber, with belfry windows on each face, all have hooded moulds and carved head-stops.

THE ALTAR

Dates from the 17th century in oak with carved rails and turned legs, there are four contemporary stools similarly carved

THE NAVE

Has plastered walls and a tiled floor. The eastern end north wall there is a doorway to a circular stair, which opens to the rood-loft. It has a four centered arch Built across the blocked north door is a Tomb recess it represents elaborate cross with three panels resting on an heraldic lion, with an upper panel showing a mans head and shoulders, with hands in prayer. The 15th century design representing drapers of trades who were in existence in Willey at that time. The wool trade was very prosperous with connections to Coventry and the Cotswold traders.

Against the chancel arch there is a modern octagonal stone Pulpit and near the south door a and a modern stone Font, Sadly, standing forlornly in the south west corner, is a 14th century disused Font with a cup shaped basin standing on a moulded capital base on a squared base. What a story of lives this could tell. This was rescued by a diligent member of the parish who found it discarded in the churchyard, no doubt dumped by workmen during the restoration they then produced the stone. Ugghh! No sense of heritage there.

THE CHANCEL

The arch is pointed of two splayed orders, the tower arch is also with three splayed orders that die out to the walls.

The roof is a good example of wooden framing timbers of 15th century workmanship, three bays wall trusses at each end, pitched low and the roof covered with lead cambered tie beams supported on curved brackets and wall posts. A delight is the richly carved Wall plates at the ends of the beams.

There are three bells, one by Hugh Watts 1617, another by Brian Eldridge 1658, third by Earye of Kettering 1730.

The PLATE has a silver Chalice and cover dated 1662. Records commence in 1661.

ADVOWSON

This is another church given away to other religious building owners. This had two virgates of land, and given to the NORMAN Abbey of Preaux between 1129-1146 when Roger Abbadon became a monk there. This was confirmed by the Earls, Roger of Warwick and Robert of Leicester, granted at the palace of the Bishop of Chester.

However this was reverted in quitclaim in 1273 by Hugh de Herdeburgh to William , Abbot of Preaux, and Nicholas prior in his cell at Warmington for a sum of 10 Marks!

During the 14th century K. Henry V made representations of the alien churches to fund his wars with France.

In 1380 annual pension of 13s 4d to Warmington Priory on the supression.

The Warmington cell must have been valuable, it was then passed to Lewis de Clifford and Thomas Erpyngham. Then finally in 1413 to the Carthusian Priory in Witham Somerset!

In 1550 the 13s 4d was reduced to 6s 8d to John Coker, to his sons Gerard, John, and Richard and their male heirs, so must have been a tidy sum for all this activity. Again the crown took control and this was in the hands of Lord Camoys in 1900. It then changed several hands, they were all eager to get their hands on this princely sum as recent as 1940. As all churches are valued this one in 1291, valued at £3 6s 8d, with the Rectory valued at £8 6s, with an addition of 7s 4d for synods and the procurations.

In conclusion this lovely church so sad, and looking drab, requiring a sum of money to cover up the weary places that sorely need the parishioners and locals to give a hand to bring it back to life. Just a little time of caring humans that have a love of heritage. This one, as you have read, has a terrific tale to tell of the way of life in medieval times.

The Earl of Denbigh is Lord of the manor.

Newnham Paddox

This place was in the possession of **Leuuinus** at the time of **K. Edward the Confessor**. As for its name it was written as feni Newbold. 'Bold' in old English is a house, this being new it followed on, and Feni was the old English way to distinguish it from all other Newbolds, to this end an ancient family Revell gave it the name. In 1086 it was a hide in Newnham (Paddox) was held of **Geoffery de Wirce by Ansegis**, who was presumably identical with 'Anseis' who held 4 hides in the adjoining parish of Harborough. From an early date it was held by a family who took their name from the place, **Roger de Newnham**, who held it of one fee under Neil de Mowbray, who is presumably the Roger, lord of Newnham, son of Aubrey, who granted land here to Monks Kirby Priory, this grant was confirmed by his son William. Phillip de Newnham, who held the fee here at the time of the death of Roger Mowbray in 1207,who died before 1222 when his widow, Julian held one third of the manor in dower. The reversion of this third was settled in 1333 on **Phillip de Newnham** (apparently grandson of the elder Phillip) and Alice his wife in tail. At the same time **Roger Ryvel** and Joan his wife settled the other two thirds of the manor on themselves for their lives, and then to Phillip and Alice in tail. In each case there were contingent remainders to Phillip's brother Robert de Newnham for life, and then to his brother John in tail, or to their sisters Joan and Mariot in tail, or to the Right heirs of Joan wife of **Roger Ryvel**, who must have been the daughter of the elder and mother of the younger Phillip.

In 1362 the Manor was held by John Colard in right of his wife Katherine, when they conveyed it to Walter Withers and Isabel his wife. From their son Ralph Withers in 1393 to John Leventhorpe, who (after an abortive conveyance to Thomas Totty) sold it on 11 November 1433 to John Fylding or **Fielding.** For it was John Fielding's grandson Sir Everard so when John died, he seized the manor of **Coldenewnham, alias Paddox Newnham** from Maurice Berkley, (representative of the Mowbrays) as it was of his manor of Melton Mowbray. It was his grandson Basil who married one of the daughters and co-heiresses of William Willington of Barcheston who died in 1585 leaving a son. Sir William. The latter's grandson, Sir William Fielding, married Susan Villiers, sister of the royal favourite of **George Duke of Buckingham,** and William was Created **BARON FIELDING** of Newnham Paddox and Viscount Fielding in 1620. On 14 September 1622 he was made **EARL of Denbigh**, his younger son George was created **Earl of Desmond** two months later. The Earl was killed in a skirmish in Birmingham on 3rd April 1643 and was succeeded by his son Basil, on whose death without issue in 1675 the estate passed to his nephew **William third Earl of Denbigh and Desmond**. It is with his direct descendants **Newnham Paddox** has remained, and is the seat of the present Earl.

POVERTY IN MEDIAEVAL ENGLAND

To understand the way the country had developed into an agricultural economy and the need to possess land, and accumulation of wealth by demands for more land and its inhabitants, by inheritance, by marriage, and fair means and foul; became the prime mover of the landed gentry. The result of this is evident today, and the pattern of development is out lined in the stories of each village in this book.

The social and economic change after the Black Death left a fragile economy of medieval peasantry where bad seasons of inclement weather and poor return of crops and livestock Left a later middle ages hardening of attitude to the peasantry, resulting making higher returns and leaving extreme poverty and a desperately poor population.

The attitudes of attempts at acquisition and retention of land by the upper class poor, lead the landed gentry to use the MANORIAL COURTS to obtain rights that were used illegally to prevent, and reduce this happening by use of the tied cottage and husbandry system. This came into force after the two plagues. This was known as the age of acquisition.

This made many landowners to seek the justice of the Royal courts to further extend their ambitions of greater economic growth, obtaining land where a person died leaving a child of low age, the crown took over and diverted to the contender usually at a price and even a title. All this in a period of great devastating poverty and destitution, leading to jealousy of acquisition of property beyond the realm of their own possessions.

This attitude brought great changes in the wool trade, by now in severe decline, to venture into other fields of trade thus creating economic poverty in the existing continental markets. The clash of traders in Coventry with those of the Cotswolds and the exports to Flanders and also the Italian manufacturers resulted in the 15th century great slump.

The arrogant, proud, and contemptuous attitude of the Landed Gentry. Brought about the lower landed middle classes eagerly reasserting their rights and enhancing of their property, just as soon as the population and the economy began to grow again in the early 16th century.

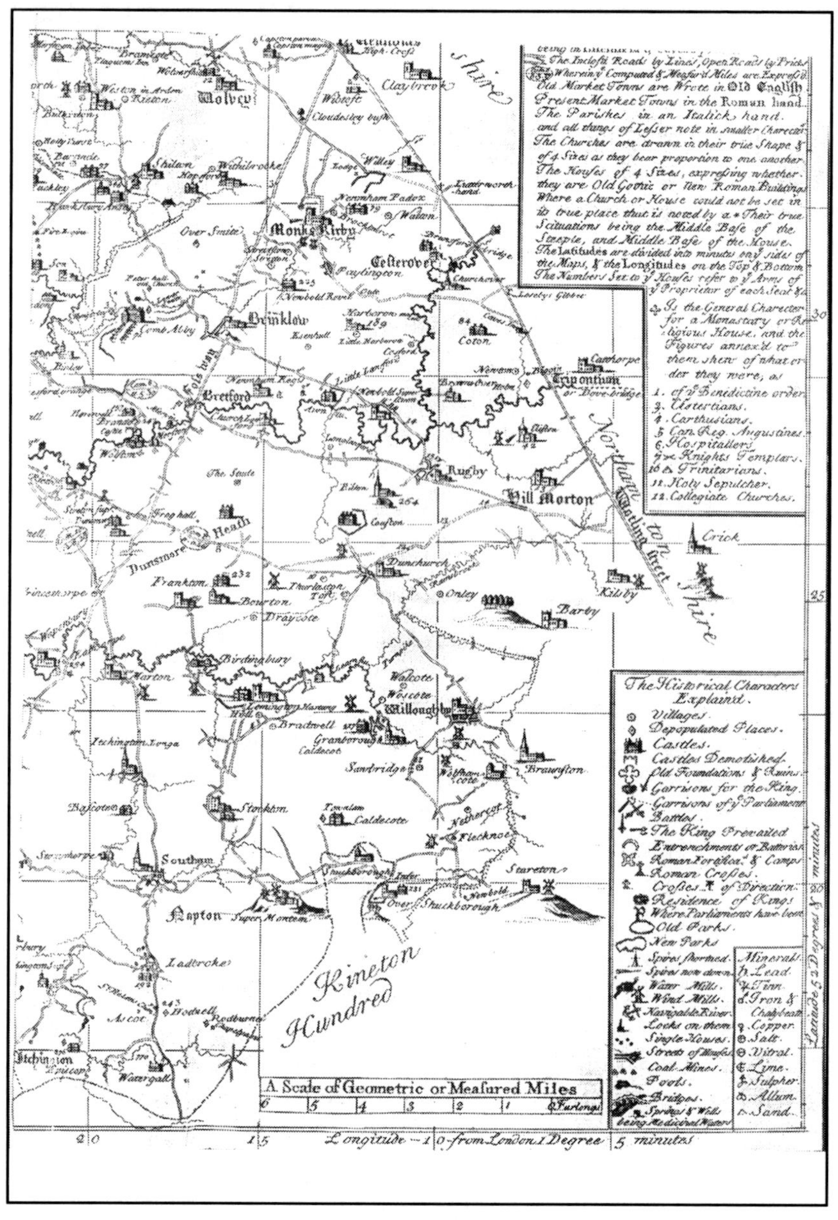

The Inclos'd Roads by Lines, Open Roads by Pricks
Whereiny Computed & Measur'd Miles are Express'd
Old Market Towns are Wrote in Old English
Present Market Towns in the Roman hand
The Parishes in an Italick hand
and all things of Lesser note in smaller Characters
The Churches are drawn in their true Shape &
of 4 Sizes as they bear proportion to one another
The Houses of 4 Sizes, expressing whether
they are Old Gothic or New Roman Buildings
Where a Church or House could not be set in
its true place that is noted by a * Their true
Scituations being the Middle Base of the
Steeple, and Middle Base of the House.
The Latitudes are divided into minutes on y sides of
the Maps, & the Longitudes on the Top & Bottom
The Numbers Set to y Houses refer to y Arms of
y Proprietor of each Seat &c
Is the General Character for a Monastary or Religious House, and the Figures annex'd to them shew of what order they were, as
1. of y Benedictine order
3. Cistertians.
4. Carthusians.
5. Con. Reg. Augustines.
6. Hospitallers.
7. Knights Templars.
10. Trinitarians.
11. Holy Sepulcher.
12. Collegiate Churches.
The Historical Characters Explain'd.
Villages.
Depopulated Places.
Castles.
Castles Demolished.
Old Foundations & Ruins.
Garrisons for the King.
Garrisons of y Parliament
Battles.
The King Prevailed
Entrenchments or Batteries
Roman Fortifica. & Camps
Roman Crosses.
Crosses of Direction.
Residence of Kings
Where Parliaments have been
Old Parks.
New Parks
Spires shortned.
Spires now down
Water Mills.
Wind Mills.
Navigable River.
Locks on them
Single Houses.
Streets of Houses
Coal Mines.
Pools.
Bridges.
Springs & Wells being Medicinal Waters
Minerals.
Lead.
Tinn.
Iron & Chalybeate
Copper.
Salt.
Vitral.
Lime.
Sulpher.
Allum.
Sand.
A Scale of Geometric or Measured Miles
6 5 4 3 2 1 Furlongs
20 15 Longitude – 10 – from London 1 Degree 5 minutes
Latitude 52 Degrees & minutes
30
25
20
Wolvey
Weston in Arden
Claybrook
High Cross
Cloudesley bush
Withibrooke
Shilton
Monks Kirby
Newnham Padox
Walton
Cesterover
Churchover
Paylington
Newbold Revel
Brinklow
Comb Abby
Coton
Bretford
Little Lawford
Tripontium or Dove bridge
Rugby
Hill Morton
Bilton
Cawston
Dunsmore Heath
Frankton
Bourton
Draycote
Dunchurch
Thurlaston
Onley
Barby
Kilsby
Crick
Birdingbury
Marton
Wolcote
Woscote
Willoughby
Bradwell
Granborough
Sawbridge
Braunston
Stockton
Caldecote
Nethercot
Flecknoe
Southam
Stareton
Shuckborough
Napton Super Montem
Ladbroke
Hodnell
Ascot
Watergall
Itchington
Kineton Hundred
Northampton shire
Watling Street

Their servile tenures continued to exercise real restraints on the increasing numbers of the peasant families, and the abuse that went hand in hand with such extreme poverty, leading to deaths of hunger and starvation that appeared not to concern the gentry.

The mean and harsh land grasping landlords, and the introduction of copyhold and the grant of the Royal courts in these cases, lead to the breakdown of tenures, (re Monks Kirby) lead to and brought about the breakdown of serfdom in England. The Nobles and gentlemen whose splendid lives depended on these villagers, labourers and towns people were considered so insignificant that to revolt was not even considered. For these persons were part of the landscape clad in coarse cloth or other cheap hand made garments, living in wattle and daub cottages, with no windows and doors, how they thought was it impossible for them to rise up when their very living depended on their conditions of employment. For them to revolt when all the gentry gave them was taken so badly. For they allowed these persons to tend their own sheep, and had small holdings, which they had to attend to if they had any energy after a very long time on the lords land. They were given a small wage for this they were expected to tend their sheep and cattle spread the dung, sow and harvest the crops, care for the birds and venison keep the woods and maintain the lords private property, provide the lords fuel, (the fact that this wage and individual holdings was not even subsistence level, just never entered into it) For the landowners this income from these properties brought great wealth. Bringing to many the hearts desire of clothes, ribbons, silks, and objects of personal and house adornment, horses, hawks, wine, and ale to entertain many people to a high standard; using the peasants as servants adorned with a badge of livery, of visiting entertainers. The even had security with armed soldiers, and knights paying by fee of loyalty.

It was not surprising that they were so out of touch with the living conditions of the poor, it came as a shock and a rude awakening that these peasants should be so ungrateful as to revolt. More so when you consider the black death of 1348-9 had decimated a third of the population, and the Statute of Labourers in 1351 had been able to give some of them a better way of life, indeed some had developed into burgesses and towns folk with a trade. (Any individual able to escape the Lords manor and stay undetected for a year and a day were now considered as freemen.) This resentment created great unrest and brought about the Peasants Revolt of 1381. Releasing Tom Ball from prison to lead them with strong words and promises that brought about country wise discontent.

In 1381 it was the poll tax of a shilling a head, (except those under 15 years, or a beggar) that was very onerous and unacceptable, when the total average wage for a year was 13 shillings and 4d!. So at first they tried soft methods of revolt it came in the form of approach to the clergy and then to the commons, which was futile since all members of the commons were either Knights, or Bugesses. So they took to lying about their ages, suddenly there were far too many under 15 years on the books so when this return gave such a small amount they took drastic action on the populace, sent officers to all to check the families personally, then demanding larger sums in return. (see Pailton)

This lead to rioting and taking matters into their own hands and three Jurors and three clerks were set on and beheaded.

This way of life now being misled by Wat Tyler, Jack Straw, and John Ball who gathered the populace on promises of better conditions and understanding they started the march in which many people were killed. The false promises and severe handling of the leaders brought a sad and pitiful end to a mild protest of the terrible conditions brought on by the ill informed and lack of understanding by the gentry.

ANCIENT TERMS EXPLAINED

A HIDE OF LAND, a term used to define areas of land which could vary, usually

60-120 acres and is equivalent of modern 30 miles.

A HUNDRED, a term used in the Doomsday book to define a Hundred and six hides.

MANOR, is a house in which a landowner could hold a Leet, or a Court, known as a Manorial Court, decided over by Court Baron.

FREE WARREN, a franchise of land conveyed as a privilege, usually by a Sovereign and subject to a promise to hold for them.

CARUCAT, Latin for a plough (Caruca), a CURRACA was a wheeled plough.

CARUATE OF LAND, as much land as one team, with eight oxen can plough in a year and a day.

VEDERER, A man employed by a large landowner, or the Sovereign, in charge of the royal forests and those in control by a landowner, he was sometimes used as a collector of tithes.

INTAIL, left by inheritance and cannot be sold, devised by will or otherwise alienated by the owner.

FREETAIL, From the Latin ' FREEODUM TALLIATUM,' meant cut short fee, the purpose was to ensure it remained intact and could not be bequeathed to an illegitimate child. So you could be wealthy in land but still in debt!

MOEITY, one of two units into which a tribe, community or family is divided, based on a unilateral descent.

TITHES, One part of a tax usually one tenth, and was often abused to its size and value.

KNIGHTS FEE, is a unit of land sufficient to provide sustenance for himself as Knight and his esquires. Also to equip and furnish his horses and armour, to be able fight for his overlord, known in loyalty as Knights Service, to maintain and conduct himself in the manner of a man of honour and chivalry.

ALIENATED, is a division or way of distancing oneself from another, which is important to them.

ENFEOFFED, a deed whereby a person was given land in exchange for a pledge of service, in terms expressed at the time.

SCUTAGE, this allowed a knight to buy himself out of the military service that he owed to his Lord.

The Blood line connection

Princess Elizabeth 1603 at Combe Abbey
to
Queen Elizabeth 2nd Great Britain

The **Stuarts Dynasty**
King James 1 = Anne of Denmark
Their daughter Elizabeth was brought up at Coombe Abbey
At 13 came to London and Married Frederick the Palatine of Bohemia becoming Queen of Bohemia (The Winter Queen)

Her 12th child Sophie married George, the Duke of Hanover becoming Electress of Hanover
Line of succession brought her first child to England

K. George 1st = Sophie Dorothea of Celle
The start of the Hanoverian Dynasty

K. George 2nd = Caroline of Brandenburgh Aspach
Frederick Lewes Prince of Wales = Augusta of Saxe-Gotha

|

K. George 3rd = Charlotte of Mecklenburg-Strelitz

K. Edward Duke of Kent = Victoria of Saxe-Coburg-Saalfeld

|

Queen Victoria = Albert of Saxe-Coburg-Saafeld

|

K. Edward VII = Alexandra of Denmark

K. George V = Mary of Teck

K. Windsor Dynasty

|

K. George VI = Lady Elizabeth Bowes-Lyon

|

Q. Elizabeth II = Prince Phillip Duke of Edinburgh

THE MONARCHS

WILLIAM I	**1066-1087**	**HOUSE OF NORMANDY**
WILLIAM RUFUS	1087-1100	
HEBRY I BEAUCLERC	1100- 1135	
STEPHEN	1135-1154	
HENRY II	**1154-1189**	**THE HOUSE OF ANJOU**
RICHARD I	1189- 1199	
JOHN	1199-1216	
HENRY III	1216-1272	
EDWARD I	1272-1307	
EDWARD II	1307-1327	
EDWARD III	1327-1377	
RICHARD II	1377-1399	
HENRY IV	1399-1413	
HENRY V	1413-1422	
HENRY VI	1422-1460	
EDWARD IV	1461-1483	
EDWARD V	1483-	
RICHARD III	1483-1485	
HENRY VII	**1485-1509**	**THE HOUSE OF TUDOR**
HENRY VIII	1509-1547	
EDWARD VI	1547-1553	
MARY I	1553-1558	
ELIZABETH I	1558-1603	
JAMES I	**1603-1625**	**THE HOUSE OF STUART**
CHARLES I	1625-1649	
CHARLES II	1660 -1685	
JAMES II	1685-1688	
MARY II	1689-1694	
WILLIAM	1689-1702	
ANNE	1702-1714	
GEORGE I	**1714-1727**	**THE HOUSE OF HANOVER**
GEORGE II	1727-1760	
GEORGE III	1760-1820	
GEORGE IV	1820-1830	
WILLIAM IV	1830-1837	
VICTORIA	1837-1901	

Sir Thomas Malory

His Story (1420-1471)

The"Le Morte D'Arthur"book, is a literary masterpiece written in Medieval times by a layman. It is Supposedly written in prison.

It is analysed being as not by a professional writer, but of an educated man.

The King Arthur's style of prose is written in the romantic speech of the writer, giving off the chivalric , moralistic, religious touch, in the manner of a writer, living at that point in time Circa 1400.

Little is known of the author except the speculation of his identity, and many dispute that it was by the man in prison. That he could speak French, Latin, and English indicated he was an educated person. It was a fact that it was written by a man in prison, and Malory was a man in prison at that time,he had been involved in the Cook Plot, and was denied a pardon. He was of Violent nature involved in several violent crimes, one of which he was involved with the riot of the poor around Combe Abbey, it said that he lead the burglary into Combe and robbed them of Gold and Silver as well as the chalice and money, and distributed amongst the poor. These chivralistic values are almost certainly the man who lived at Newbold Revel, and of the Malory family who held ground there.

Thomas Malory was born 1400 app. The son of John Malory of that manor and his wife Phillipa Chetwynd. John Malory was a retainer of the Lord lieutenant of France, Richard Beauchamp Earl of Warwick and was on campaign with him in the siege of Calais 1414, and had possessions there, at the fall of Calais he lost these properties and returned to Newbold Revel in 1439. He died in that year.

Thomas was knighted and became Sir Thomas Malory, inheriting considerable wealth and grounds around Monks Kirby and in this area of Warwickshire. Becoming involved with politics in 1445 and became an MP. Involving himself in many unfair clashes, Coombe Abbey, Duke of Buckinghams estates, raids on the Peto lands, and raids in Essex. His enemies sought to blacken his name branding him a 'Rapist, Church robber, extortioner, and would be murderer'. He was a swashbuckling figure with a knightly attitude of days when knights were bold. He volunteered for military service in Northumbria buying back the political favours, but finally the Cook conspiracy swept him to gaol.

It was here that he gained eternal fame writing the famous literary masterpiece "Le Morte DeArthur" He died in Newgate prison.

On the 12th of March 1471 he was buried nearby in the church of St, Francis, a Marble tomb reads, *"Dominus Thomas Mallare Valens Miles Obitt 14 mar 1470 De parochial Monkenkybrby in comitatu Wawici"*

Note; there have been recent discoveries and with evidence confirming that it was indeed, Sir Thomas Mallore, from Newbold Revel, who wrote the book.

The Lord of the Manor

Earl of Denbigh

William Fielding was created Baron Fielding, of Newnham Paddox, and also Viscount Fielding in 1620.

The title Earl was created in 1622 for the courtier and soldier, William Fielding, 1st Viscount Fielding, for he was master of the Great Wardrobe under King James 1st and he also took part in the 1625 expedition to Cadiz. His second son, the Hon. George Fielding was created Earl of Desmond in 1628.

Unlike his father he fought as a Parliamentarian in the Civil War. In 1664 he was created Baron St. Liz in the peerage of England, with remainder to the heir's male of his father

Lord Denbigh was succeeded by his eldest son the second Earl.

He died childless and was succeeded by his nephew, William Fielding.2nd. Earl of Desmond, who now became the third Earl of Denbigh, (he also succeeded in the barony of St, Liz according to the second remainder) His son, the Fourth Earl, served as Lord-Lieutenant of Leicestershire and Denbighshire. His great-great- grandson, the seventh Earl (the titles having descended from father to son, with the exception for the seventh Earl who succeeded his grandfather), was a soldier and courtier. His grandson, the Ninth Earl, served as Lord-in -waiting (government whip in the house of Lords from 1897-1905 in the Conservative administrations of Lord Salisbury and Arthur Balfour.) Since 2010 the titles are held by his great-great-great-grandson, the twelfth Earl, who succeeded his father in 1995 (the titles having descended from father to son, with the exception for the tenth Earl who succeeded his grandfather). LORD DENBIGH IS GRAND CARVER OF ENGLAND!

The Hon. George Fielding, second son of the first Earl of Denbigh was created Baron Fielding, of Lecaghe in the county of Tipperary, and Viscount Callan, of Callan in the County of Kilkenny, in 1662, and was made Earl of Desmond in 1628. All three titles were in the Peerage of Ireland.

He was succeeded by his son the second Earl, who in 1675 succeeded his uncle as third Earl of Denbigh.

Other members of the family worth mentioning such as the writer Henry Fielding

(Who spelt his name differently) was the son of Edmund Fielding, the third son of John Fielding, the youngest son of the 3rd Earl. His sister Sarah Fielding was also a well-known author. Their half-brother (Edmund's son by a different wife) was John Fielding. Lady Elizabeth Fielding, daughter of the first Earl of Denbigh, was created Countess of Guildford for life in 1660.

The Hon. Sir Percy Robert Basil Fielding, second son of the seventh Earl, was a general in the Army.

Alexander Stephen Rudolph Fielding, is the present Earl of Denbigh and

11th Earl Desmond. His wife is the Countess Suzy.

The heir apparent is the present holder's son Peregrine Rudolph Henry Fielding, Viscount Fielding.

The family seat is at Newnham Paddox, it has the one of the finest gates in the land, crafted by British hands and influenced by the Italian designs. Landscaped by Capability Brown and a delight to the eye at every turn of the head.

It is open to visitors and many events are being staged there.

Note; The present Earl of Denbigh can trace his lineage back from the same area and time that the present Queen Elizabeth is able to do so.

Lightning Source UK Ltd.
Milton Keynes UK
UKOW050020161112

202269UK00007B/52/P

9 781782 220275